101 WAYS
TO PREPARE
A HOT DOG

by Frank Furter

MIDDLE COAST PUBLISHING

"Good books are where we find our dreams."

101 Ways to Prepare a Hot Dog
by Frank Furter
ISBN-13: 978-0934523-26-4

Editor@Middle-Coast-Publishing.com

Cover credit, Regional favourite hot dogs, by permission of the
National Hot Dog and Sausage Council.

This book will change your life. The days of plopping a hot dog on a bun, squirting a squiggle of mustard on it and calling it lunch are over. . .

Cooked hot dog with mustard garnish, by Czar, public domain.

When King George VI and Queen Elizabeth of England visited President and Mrs. Franklin D. Roosevelt at their estate in Hyde Park, New York, in the summer of 1939, they picnicked on hot dogs.

MENU

RECIPES

"The only movie Hollywood ever made about a hot dog was an Oscar Weiner. . . ." Frank Furter - Cannes, France

EXACTLY WHAT IS A HOT DOG?

In 1913 the Coney Island, New York, Chamber of Commerce banned the use of the term hot dog on restaurant signs on its island, an action prompted by concerns about foreign visitors taking the term literally and mistakenly assume dog meat was in the sausage. Because of this word ban, immigrants passing through the area didn't come to know a sausage on a bun as a hot dog. Instead, the ubiquitous handheld food became known as a Coney Island. Notice we didn't call it a sandwich.

Frankfurter content is regulated by Federal law. Traditional hot dogs are made from beef, pork, veal, chicken or turkey and are available with, or without, natural-casing skins. Hot dogs contain up to 30-percent fat and 10-percent added water. Hot dog sizes range from tiny, cocktail wieners up to the venerable foot-long. Most common is the six-inch length sold in grocery stores in 16 ounce packs of eight.

HOW TO HEAT A HOT DOG

What's the best way to heat a hot dog? Notice that we didn't say cook a hot dog. That's because hot dogs are already cooked. All that's required is to heat them by grilling, steaming or boiling. Restated for emphasis, no matter which method is chosen, one heats a hot dog, but does not cook it. For best results, heat low and slow.

Technically, hot dogs are ready to eat right out of the package. But to avoid the possibility of listeria the United States Department of Agriculture sagely advises: "Before eating, heat hot dogs until steaming hot." Which means an internal temperature of 155° Fahrenheit. When served at a temperature cooler than 140° F, tepid hot dogs are spongy with little flavor. While a temperature higher than 165° F bursts them wide open and dries them out. This holds true for both skinless and natural-casing hot dogs.

Suffice it to say a hot dog that has burst its casing is a sign of operator error: Split down the middle, or bulging, means it's been heated at too high of a temperature. To prevent a hot dog from doing the splits, poke a few holes in it with a fork or the tip of a sharp knife. As the fat in the hot dog cooks, it emits steam. The holes allow the steam to escape. And don't reheat yesterday's hot dog. Instead, consider grinding it or chopping it up and putting it in chili or Coney Dog sauce. More on the latter later.

STEAMING

Steam in either a Dutch oven, or a Chicken Fryer fitted with a steamer rack, or a bamboo steamer. Fill the pan with enough water to reach just below the steamer rack, but not above that level. Furthermore, liquid should not bubble up onto the hot dogs. Bring the water to a rolling boil, reduce the heat to low, and then arrange the hot dogs in the steamer basket. Cover tightly and steam for five to seven minutes, or until the hot dogs are heated clear through.

To steam buns, simply stack them on top of the dogs during the last two minutes. Or, in the alternative, warm the buns in a strainer or straining pot lid placed on top of the pot.

POACHING/BOILING

Gently poaching hot dogs in water uniformly warms them to the optimum temperature of 155° F. By this method, heat water in a saucepan over high heat, monitoring the progression with a thermometer. When the temperature bumps 150° F to 155° F, lower the heat to a slight simmer. Place the dogs in the water to warm, making sure there is enough water to completely submerge the hot dog. Once again monitoring the temperature, warming uncovered for up to 20 minutes, or until the hot dogs float.

Remove with tongs and place on a paper towel to dry. Be mindful not to leave them soaking in the water them too long or they will pick up an off-flavor from the metal pan. Street vendors call poached hot dogs dirty water dogs.

A poaching liquid of beer and hot-dog onions or sauerkraut infuses franks with lots of extra flavor. Another worthy option is a water bath speckled with black peppercorns, mustard seed, red pepper flakes and bay leaf.

A well-known trick among savvy hot dog cart vendors is to drop a beef bouillon cube, or the contents of a can of beer, into the boiling water to saturate it with flavor and at the same time prevent the water from leaching out the flavor of the dogs. A single garlic clove makes for another flavorful addition.

Know that larger natural-casing dogs are best when grilled because when boiled, they're more chewy than snappy. Also important to know, hot dogs split and burst when boiled too long.

Warmed hot dogs do not hold well. Serve immediately or the skins turn tough and start to wrinkle and shrivel.

THE TWO-STEP HEATING METHOD

Another method worthy of consideration heats in two-steps. First, poach the dog. Second, place it on the grill at high heat. Dogs char in mere seconds. Remove them the moment they show color. By this method the hot dog maintains plump juiciness from the poach and at the same time reveals the pleasant aesthetics of lightly, seared surface from the grill or broiler.

MICROWAVING

The problem with a microwave oven is that it heats unevenly. One end of the hot dog will measure a relatively cool 150° F, while the other end is overcooked at 180° F. Which is exactly the reason why aficionados recommend only heating hot dogs in a microwave if no other heating method is available.

To its advantage, microwaving a hot dog takes but a couple of minutes, while any of the other methods take from 20 minutes to a half of an hour. Also on the plus side of the balance sheet, while frozen dogs take longer to cook, a hot dog coming out of the freezer takes less than a minute to heat.

Tip: Cut thin slits along the length of your dog to allow air to escape so the hot dogs do not explode. Place in a microwave-safe bowl and cover in water. Warm for two or three minutes, and then let cool for 30 seconds. The water bath better distributes the heat throughout the entire length of the hot dog.

An alternative microwave method is to tightly wrap the hot dog in a paper towel, dutifully folding the ends under the dog in order to keep them closed. Place the wrapped hot dog on a plate and microwave for 30- to 45-seconds, or until heated through.

OVER A ROARING CAMPFIRE

Heating hot dogs over a campfire is as easy as poking the hot dogs onto the sharp end of a stick and holding it over the campfire. Regularly rotate the hot dog to warm it evenly throughout. S'mores will doubtlessly follow.

DEEP FRIED

A deep-fried hot dog is affectionately known as a ripper for the violence scalding hot oil wreaks upon it, opening up a great, yawning chasm along its length, albeit one that's perfect home for a zigzagging squiggle of yellow mustard or a dollop of glistening, green relish.

Thicker dogs work best. Wrap each one with a strip of bacon pinned in place with a toothpick. Refrigerate the wrapped hot dogs while heating the oil to a temperature of 375° F. This lofty temperature is necessary so that the majority of the frying happens at around 350° F. The chilled temperature of the refrigerated dogs going into the oil bath lowers the temperature. Place the dogs in the oil and fry to the level of crispiness desired. The longer it's left bubbling in the oil, the crispier its outside.

Know that hot dogs dunked in frying oil immediately sink to the bottom of the kettle. When they rise like a Phoenix to the top, they are called an in-and-outer. Heated for a minute or two longer makes for a medium ripper. Heated yet another minute or two makes a Weller, a well-done hot dog. Five minutes in the oil makes for a crispy outside with a tender, juicy inside. Fried even longer, until the hot dog sports a pattern of black spots, qualifies it as a Cremator. Left in the fryer for eight to 10 minutes renders a hot dog extremely well done, inside and out, crispy with the texture of bacon. Tastes vary.

CROCK POT/SLOW COOKER

Use a Slow Cooker to get hot dogs to the temp around 160° F and hold at that temperature. No water is required because the hot dogs cook in their own juices, crisping the skin, but staying moist and juicy inside. When stewed in hot water for too long they would split. Naturally the size of the crock-pot and the number of hot dogs loaded into it affect how long it takes to bring the hot dogs up to their proper temperature.

To heat eight to 16 hot dogs in a crock-pot: Place the hot dogs into the slow cooker and arranged with space in between. Where the hot dogs make contact with the crock-pot surface the hot dogs will turn brown and crispy.

Warm on High, but don't make the rookie mistake of taking off the lid to sneak a peek, or precious heat escapes, increasing the time needed to warm the hot dogs. Warm for one to two hours, or until hot and slightly browned. When the hot dogs reach an internal temperature of 160° F, reduce to Low, or the Hold setting, until it is time to serve. Before serving, make sure those dog huddled in the middle are fully hot

OVEN ROASTED

Oven roasting, or baking, results in juicy, blackened hot dogs with a flavor as close as you can get to grilled hot dogs, albeit without the inconvenience of lighting the grill. Another benefit, oven-roasted hot dogs boast a pleasant flavor, especially when baked right alongside French fries or baked potatoes destined to join the hot dogs on the dinner plate.

Preheat the oven to 425° F. In the beginning slice lengthwise down each side of the hot dog. But be careful not slice clear through the hot dogs. Instead, make just enough of a cut to vent steam from the insides.

Place the roasting pan in the oven and heat the hot dogs, dutifully rolling them over during the baking process in order to ensure even warming. Bake hot dogs for 10 minutes at 425° F. Be on the lookout for the skin to begin to brown and the dogs to beginning to curl. For a crispy texture, first briefly brown the hot dog under the broiler. Add cheese, if desired and place the hot dogs back in the oven for an additional minute.

Or, insert a sliver of pickle and a sliver of high-temperature cheese like Raclette inside a slit hot dog. Wrap it with a strip of bacon secured with toothpicks. Bake until the bacon is crispy and the cheese is melted.

GRILLING

When using a charcoal grill, burn the briquettes for 30 to 45 minutes, or until the coals ash over, then spread them out over the bottom of the grill.

Place **natural-casing hot dogs** on the grill rack and heat for three to four minutes until charred, but not blackened. More particularly, grill a hot dog over medium, indirect heat, away from the grill's hottest spot. Watch carefully. Turn frequently. Hot dogs brown quickly. As soon as one side starts to brown, turn it over. In your mind's eye, imagine the hot dog as having a square shape and turn four times to brown all four sides. Two to three minutes per side is about right, with a total heating time ranging from eight to 12 minutes. Before grilling, consider dipping natural-casing hot dogs in milk to add a crunch to the skin.

Grill **skinless hot dogs** until they begin to char, toughening the exterior so it snaps similar to a natural casing. Also know that skinless hot dogs better absorb smoke flavor. Heat the gas grill to its hottest setting. Just before grilling, lower the heat to Medium (about 400° F).

An old Chicago hot dog-cart trick cross-cuts the ends, or makes a progression of diagonal cuts lengthwise prior to grilling. X-pattern cuts on opposite sides of the hot dog obviates the specter of shriveled skinless hot dogs. The reason for this maneuver is as simple as the sea is salt. **Skinless hot dogs** look plump and juicy while grilling. But once removed from heat, they deflate and shrivel. That's because the center was moist, but around the edges it had begun to dry out and exhibit a papery, leathery exterior that adds the undesirable trait of chew instead of snap.

Moreover, warming **slashed** hot dogs on the grill spreads the slits wide open, allowing heat to more quickly penetrate to the center, shortening cooking time. Skinless hot dogs cooked in this manner stay plump and juicy and don't shrivel. Instead, they blossom, opening up like pine cones. The crosshatch, when combined with a ketchup-based marinade that seeps into the crevices, glazes the hot dog with sugary-spicy flavor, giving greater opportunity for the surface to come in contact with a searing-hot grill grate and leaves the hot dog with lots of little charred and crispy bits for the best blistered effect.

Take this concept to the next higher level by spiral-cutting a hot dog. Impale it with a kebab stick or bamboo skewer and make a long, spiraling cut deep along the entire length. The spiral cut looks snazzy. Beyond mere aesthetics, it adds crispiness by increasing the hot dog's surface area. Perhaps most important of all, spiraling expands the surface area for the condiments to better mingle. Pull out the stick, then heat. That said: Beware! It's also easier to overcook and dry out a hot dog this way.

CONDIMENTS

There are a myriad of options for topping hot dogs. Beyond the ubiquitous mustard, relish, or ketchup. Keep in mind it is not wise to pile ingredients onto a hot dogs like the pizza. Carefully consider the condiments, but that said, there is no need to be sparse in the selection.

There is but one, essential rule for hot dog condiments. There must be at least one acidic or vinegary condiment in the mix.

That's because hot dogs, being high in fat content, rely on something astringent and acidic for flavour balance. Options include either jarred or homemade relish, finely chopped raw white onion, spicy brown mustard, or classic yellow mustard. With mustard, remember to shake the bottle before squeezing to avoid that first pathetic spurt of faintly yellow, mustard water.

Generally, in the West, folks like jalapeño peppers on a hot dog.

In the Midwest it's ketchup.

In the Northeast it's sauerkraut.

In the South it's chili, cheese and coleslaw.

With that in mind, always dress the dog, not the bun. Apply condiments in the following order: First, mustard and chili, followed by chunky condiments like relish, onions and sauerkraut, followed by shredded cheese, followed by spices, like celery salt or pepper.

Evenly distribute the toppings so there is a taste of each ingredient with every bite. Squirt the mustard directly onto the hot dog from one end to the other in an artistic zigzag pattern. Add a generous amount of sweet relish. Onions go on top of the hot dog; the amount depends on personal preference. Place tomatoes along the gap between the top of the bun and the hot dog. Place the pickle spear, or slice, in the gap between the bottom of the bun and the hot hog. Lastly, sprinkle a dash of celery salt or other spice.

As for, gulp, ketchup on a hot dog:

"Nobody, I mean nobody, puts ketchup on a hot dog."

So said Clint Eastwood in the role of Dirty Harry Callahan in the movie Sudden Impact. Moreover, the National Hot Dog and Sausage Council's Hot Dog Etiquette suggests that no one over the age of 18 should never eat ketchup on a hot dog because it sweetness and acidic flavour overpowers the wiener muting its flavor.

A FEW WORDS ABOUT MUSTARD

When Americans think of mustard, in their mind's eye they see bright-yellow mustard. But the reality is that there are hundreds of different kinds of mustard in the world, and not just school bus yellow. Some of the most common are Dijon, spicy brown, coarse, whole grain, and horseradish.

Mustard, one of the most ancient of spices, is blended from mustard seeds harvested from a wide variety of mustard plants, essentially the plant's flowers. The darker the seed, the spicier its flavour. Conversely, the lighter the colour, the milder its flavour. The appeal of mustard to the palate is the way it adds dimension and depth to the flavor of a hot dog without masking it.

The Ancient Romans are credited with being the first to experiment with mustard paste as a condiment. They mixed unfermented grape juice (the must) with ground mustard seeds (called *sinapis*) to make burning must, *mustum ardens* — hence must ard (sic).

Earlier civilizations, notably China and Egypt, used whole mustard seeds. Restated for emphasis, they used the whole seeds, not ground seeds, as spice. During the medieval period in European history, mustard was medicine and also used as a condiment to flavor bland food.

The most commonly used mustard in the United States of America is the familiar **American Yellow Mustard**. American mustard dresses hot dogs, sandwiches, pretzels and hamburgers and is also an ingredient of many potato salads, barbecue sauces, salad dressings and tuna salad. It is affectionately referred to as ballstyle mustard incorporates horseradish which makes it even spicier than spicy brown. A variety popular in Louisiana called Creole Mustard is significantly coarser than Spicy Brown.

Whole-grain mustard, also known as granary mustard, mixes whole seeds with other ingredients. Different flavors and strengths are created through blends of mustard seed species. **Groningen Mustard** is an example of mustard with partially ground grains.

It should come as no big surprise to learn **Honey Mustard** blends mustard and honey, typically mixed in a one to one ratio. Commonly used on sandwiches and as a dip for chicken nuggets, it can also be combined with vinegar or olive oil to make salad dressing. But its very existence gives rise to the question whether this sweet condim park mustard.

The term **Hot Mustard** describes mustards using pungent black or brown mustard seeds rather than the white mustard seeds used to make milder mustards.

Bright yellow in color and with a thicker consistency than the mild American mustard, **English Mustard** is one of the hottest in the world. It stings the tongue and burns the nose. The most famous brand is Colman's, first produced in 1814 as a powder in its distinctively yellow tin.

The famous Grey Poupon mustard, known as **Dijon**, has been a center of mustard-making for nearly a millennium. It is traditionally made with stone-ground brown mustard and verjus, the tart juice of unripe grapes. In contemporary times Dijon mustard substitutes white wine for verjus. While mustard factories still operate in Dijon and adjoining towns, most Dijon mustard is manufactured elsewhere. Even Dijon mustard produced in France is made nearly exclusively from Canadian mustard seed.

The two most famous German mustards are **Düsseldorf** and **Bavarian Sweet Mustard**. The main difference between these two is that Bavarian Sweet Mustard remains true to its namesake. Bavarian sweet mustard contains very little acid, substituting copious amounts of sugar for preservation. While Düsseldorf has more of a sweet-sour taste.

Spirited Mustards are made with alcoholic spirits. Variations include Arran mustards with whiskey, brandied peach mustard, Cognac mustard, Irish pub mustard blended with whiskey and Jack Daniel's mustard. **Beer Mustard** replaces vinegar with beer.

Irish Mustard is whole-grain mustard seed blended with either Irish Whiskey (of course Irish), stout (commonly Guinness) and/or honey.

Spicy Brown Mustard is common in the United States, its seeds coarsely ground, lending a speckled, brownish-yellow colour. Already spicier than mere American yellow mustard, some Deli-ent an appropriate choice for hot dogs? The answer depends on one's taste buds.

Hot Pepper Mustard - Chili peppers of various strengths are used to make a variety of mustards more piquant than plain mustard. Peppers or hot sauce made from peppers are added to mustards of different base styles such as yellow mustard, brown mustard or spirited mustards.

Hot Table Mustard may easily be prepared by the home cook by mixing ground mustard seed, turmeric and wheat flour to the desired consistency with water or an acidic liquid such as wine, vinegar, or beer, and leaving it stand for about ten minutes. It is usually prepared immediately before a meal. Know that mustard prepared with water is more pungent, but deteriorates rapidly.

Russian Mustard is sharp and spicy-hot, prepared from a blend of Indian mustard seed, salt, sugar, vegetable oil and high acid content, distilled white vinegar (a 6- to 9%-solution as opposed to table vinegar's 5% acidity).

Mustard flour is diluted with hot water in Russia, resulting in more efficient allyl isothiocyanate production lending a sharper taste. Indian mustard has less heat-sensitive glucosinolates, so unlike other varieties of seed, hot water does not reduce its pungency. A final word: Mustard can make or break a good hot dog recipe.

LOW-COUNTRY BARBECUE SAUCE

Not all barbecue sauces are red in colour. In fact, South Carolina Mustard BBQ Sauce is a bright yellow, mustard-based sauce that tastes as delicious as any vinegar or tomato-based sauce. This class of mustard sauces can be simple or complex, but must-have ingredients include: Yellow mustard, vinegar, sugar and onions. While brown sugar, apple cider vinegar, dry mustard and cayenne pepper are common options.

Know that barbecue sauces mature while they cook, meaning they needs to simmer for at least 30 minutes. When holding for hours, add a little more mustard and water to keep it pourable. The pungent flavors deepen with age, so prepare the sauce at least a day ahead of time. Slather on sauce early in the warming process in order to better caramelize the sugar. Keeping in mind the short warming time required for hot dogs, paint on sauces in a succession of coats, letting each layer coat caramelize in turn.

THE BEST CHEESES FOR HOT DOGS

Without belaboring the point, here are some notes on cheese and hot dogs. You already know the cheese may be on the bun, on the wiener, or the hot dogs proper can be split and its middle stuffed with blue cheese, cheddar or whatever flavour suites your taste buds.

Raclette is a semi-hard cow's milk cheese commonly used for melt-ability, the chief characteristic that makes it a perfect condiment for hot dogs. So too is warm cream cheese for the way it spreads so easily atop a hot dog. Danish Havarti, a butter cheese, bridges the gap between being spreadable and super easy to melt, kind of sorta like Raclette.

Swiss cheese's mild flavor, along with its firm and stretchy texture, are perfect for melting Be advised that while a good quality Swiss cheese melts great, lesser quality wedges tend to be oily.

Moreover, there's no argument that blue cheese with its spider web of Bleu veins is crumbly and stinks. But when blended with other cheeses like Pepper Jack, or with crumbled bacon, it finds a happy home on a hot dog.

In our test kitchen, and with years of experience enjoying hot dogs, we learned that sharp cheddar is the go-to cheese for restaurant grilled-cheeses sandwiches and on hot dogs.

Want white? Buy either expensive or Kraft. Either way, heated white cheese gets oozy but still manages to hold together well enough to eat without it dripping all over hands and shirt. And say what you will about American cheese, but there can be no argument that it tastes delicious on a hot dog.

THE PICKLE

Choose kosher dill spears from the refrigerated section of the grocery store, rather than the aisle along with the canned goods. Those jars of pickles are mushy and lack snap. Hot dog aficionados believe the snap of the pickle is every bit as important as the snap of the hot dog and therefore refrigerated pickles are a prerequisite.

THE BUN

The bun can be anything from a common potato roll to French bread. Toasted buns add the advantage of lending a more stable platform that doesn't fall apart as easily while taking healthy bites. Also, generously slathering it in butter before toasting improves its flavor. Consider garlic butter.

"A hot dog at the ball park is better than steak at the Ritz."
Humphrey Bogart

AMERICANIZED HOT DOGS

It's no secret Mexican and Chinese restaurants don't always serve authentic ethnic food. Truth be told, all too often they serve Tex-Mex or Americanized Chinese. With that reality in mind, and served up with a big dollop of poetic license, here are an assortment of fanciful hot dog variations from around the world that we dreamed up in our test kitchen.

France - Roasted garlic and Fontina cheese chicken-sausage dressed with saffron Dijonnaise and *formager d'affinoise*. Or the Cordon Bleu, a grilled frank laid down on top of sliced ham, a slice of Swiss cheese and a couple of dabs of Dijon mustard.

In our mind's eye we see the Parisian Hot Dog topped with crumbled (not melted) Bleu cheese, marinated red onions and tomatoes served on a croissant. The Monte Cristo Dog, replete with its French toast bun loaded with a hot dog, a single slice of ham and turkey followed by grated Swiss cheese and then back on the grill for a minute or so to melt the cheese before dressing it with a drizzle of maple syrup.

Germany - A big, fat hot dog dressed with a helping of sauerkraut and a sprinkling of pretzel bits, or in the alternative, with a slice of aged Cheddar cheese and the works liberally smeared with Dusseldorf mustard

Greece – A hot dog dressed with *tzatziki*, cucumber and Kalamata olives, or a hot dog topped with herbed Feta cheese, black olives and onions The Kalamata olives would be both chopped green and mixed with cream cheese then spread on a grilled frankfurter.

Korea – A hot dog dressed with Asian mustard, Kimchi, and thinly-sliced red onion.

Italy – A skinless hot dog skewered with numerous, long threads of spaghetti, poking out both ends, boiled until the pasta is al dente, then served on a plate and drizzled with either pasta sauce or pizza sauce.

Japan – A hot dog dressed with Wasabi mayonnaise, a sprinkle of Asian snack mix and pickled ginger.

Mexico – A hot dog dressed with a big dollop of guacamole purée and some salsa.

Polynesian - Hot dog dressed with Hoisin Sauce, pineapple, and scallions.

Spain – A hot dog dressed with a healthy schmear of Pimiento cheese spread, a bit of Serrano ham and some Manchego cheese.

Sweden – A hot dog smeared with a dollop of Lingonberry Jam and liberally dressed with caramelized onions and topped with a ladle of hot gravy.

Tex-Mex – A hot dog topped with salsa, Monterey Jack cheese, and chopped jalapeño peppers.

Thailand – A hot dog topped with peanut sauce, shredded carrot and a taste of cilantro.

Vietnamese Dog - Dressing a hot dog *bánh mì* -style (Vietnamese sandwich) with quick-pickled daikon radishes, carrots, cucumbers, fresh cilantro, mint, and sriracha mayo lends a fresh, bright flavor.

FROM OUR TEST KITCHEN

A Real Dilly of a Dog - Season a hot dog with a couple of sprinkles of fresh dill, lay on a slice of Provolone cheese, followed by sautéed mushrooms and grilled onions.

Bagel Dogs - Spread a thin layer of cream cheese over a split bun with a natural casing dog inside that's already been warmed. Pop the whole mess in a toaster oven to render the cream cheese melty.

Barbecue Hot dog – A frankfurter grilled with tangy barbecue sauce and dressed with hot peppers that only moments before were cooked on the grill alongside the hot dog.

Bleu Cheese Frank - Hot dog liberally garnished with crumbled Bleu cheese (not melted) and a generous sprinkling of bacon bits.

BLT - A hot dog prepared a la BLT (Bacon Lettuce and Tomato sandwich), which is to say dressed with bacon bits, or slices, lettuce, tomato and mayonnaise and of course served on toast.

Blue Moon Melty - A grilled frankfurter topped with melted Bleu cheese, sautéed mushrooms, lettuce and tomato chunks served on a grilled bun

Cajun Frankfurter - a Cajun blackened hot dog with a slice of Colby Jack cheese melted over it, served on a sesame bun and dressed with Creole mayonnaise, onions and tomatoes.

Cheesy Pizza Dog - Hot dog slathered with pizza sauce, and of course, the full complement of Provolone and Mozzarella cheeses.

Chuck Wagon - Pile pinto beans high as the prairie sky on the hot dog, along with bacon, chilies and cheddar cheese. Serve on a toasted potato bun. Toasting a bun helps it stay together with the load of beans.

Fajitas - Lengthwise slices of hot dog, as opposed to rounds, sprinkled with fajita seasoning after being laid down in a doubled thickness tortilla, then dressed with small cubes of guacamole, sour cream, shredded lettuce, diced tomatoes and salsa.

Five-Spice Heaven - This would be the venerable hot dog seasoned with Chinese five-spice powder, grilled and served with

17

a soy-ginger sauce dip.

French Onion Dog - On top of a frankfurter warming on the grill (indirect heat) spread a goodly amount of caramelized onions and either grated Swiss cheese or Gruyère cheese. Let the cheese melt. Sprinkle on fresh thyme. Serve on a toasted bun.

Horseradish Garlic Dog – Top a dog with onions, garlic and horseradish. Fear not vampires.

Jalapeno Hot Dog - Grilled frankfurter seasoned with diced jalapeno peppers and a splash of hot pepper sauce. Top with melted cheddar *and* cream cheese.

Just Corny - Garnish a grilled hot dog on a toasted bun with a big dollop of tangy corn relish (red pepper, corn, white vinegar, ground red pepper, salt and green onions).

La Trattoria Napoli – Long, thin slices of hot dog laid down alongside thin strips of roasted red bell peppers and grated Mozzarella cheese. Serve on Focaccia bread schmeared with pesto mayonnaise.

Lone Star State Red Dog - Serve a grilled hot dog open-faced and smothered with chili, cheddar and Monterey jack cheeses and grilled onion.

Meatza - A hot dog split open before grilling and its slit stuffed with a thin strip of Mozzarella cheese and given a squiggle of pizza sauce and a couple rounds of pepperoni. After heating, it's topped with diced tomatoes and bacon bits.

My Big Fat French Onion Dip Dog - Slather a mess of French onion dip onto a hot dog, already set in a bun, followed by a handful of crushed potato chips and a sprinkling of sliced green onions or chives.

My Blue Bayou - A grilled frankfurter link sprinkled with crumbled Bleu cheese (again, not melted), tomato, lettuce and hot pepper mayonnaise.

Not Yo' Dog – Simply dress a dog with refried beans, Longhorn cheddar and a sprinkling of crumbled nachos.

Old Hickory - Cover a frankfurter with a big, thick slide of cheddar cheese, a slice of bacon and hickory barbecue sauce

Olive Pizza Dog - Before grilling, split a hot dog along its entire length and stuff the slit with a thin slice of mozzarella cheese. Cover dog and cheese with pizza sauce as well as a sprinkling of black and also green olive rounds.

Omelet Dogger - Grilled lengthwise slices of hot dog, along with a generous portion of diced ham, dressed with a slice of Cheddar cheese, mushrooms and green peppers, served on a toasted English muffin

Onion Dog - A grilled frankfurter laid down in a bun and sprinkled with both grilled and raw onions. That's it. No other condiments.

Piña Colada - A grilled frankfurter dressed with melted Brick cheese, pineapple chunks and shredded coconut

Poor Man's Stroganoff – Top a hot dog with a thin slice of Swiss cheese, dress with sour cream, grilled onions and mushrooms.

Reubenesque - Melt Swiss cheese on grilling hot dog, place in a bun, then splash on a goodly quantity of Thousand Island dressing and finally lay on a couple big dollops of a coleslaw

Salsa Taco Dog - Top a grilled frank with shredded lettuce, tomato, sour cream, black olives and salsa. It's the ultimate walking taco

Simply Worcestershire – This is nothing more complicated than a mess of hot dogs smothered in a heap of mushrooms previously sautéed in Worcestershire sauce.

Smokey Dog - Top a hot dog with roasted, balsamic onions, grilled bacon and smoked cheese. So easy.

Spicy Jack - Melt Jack cheese melted on a frankfurter dressed with jalapeno peppers and onions.

Texas Tough – Season a hot dog with a few sprinkles of hot sauce and a handful of dried red peppers, smother it under a blanket of pepper cheese and barbecue sauce. Served on thick Texas Toast, of course!

Texican - Pile a goodly quantity of guacamole chunks, onions and bacon bits (or a single slice) on the hot dog.

The Beef Lover - A grilled hot dog topped with small chunks of roast beef, dressed with horseradish, served on an onion roll. Muenster cheese is optional.

The Cowboy Way - Dress a hot dog with grilled mushrooms, grilled onion, bacon and Monterey Jack cheese.

The Islander - Smother a hot dog with Thousand Island dressing, or in the alternative, salsa rosada, followed by lettuce, tomato and pickles.

The Skunk - Dress a warm hot dog (warmed for easier spreading) with peanut butter (no matter whether it's chunky or creamy), marshmallow fluff and chocolate sauce.

The Tiki Hut - Wrap one or two slices of bacon around a hot dog and pin in place with toothpicks. When done grilling, brush with teriyaki sauce. Serve in a toasted bun topped then dressed with diced grilled pineapple, chopped red onion, and another drizzle of teriyaki sauce. Alternatively, chunk the hot dog and skewer it along with chunks of pineapple.

Tortilla Flats – Two soft tortilla shells back to back, populated by one or two grilled frankfurters, dressed with tomato, onion, oregano, basil, both mozzarella and Parmesan cheeses, and wrapped up tight tighter than an idiot's watch.

Walla Walla – Thinly sliced hot dogs pan-fried in a sweet & sour chutney comprised of sautéed white onions, raisins, mustard seed and Marsala wine. Serve on big, thick, slices of Texas toast

REGIONAL HOT DOGS VARIETIES
BY STATE AND CITY

ALABAMA

The Willy Dog is a pinkish-red hot dog topped with ketchup, mustard, chili, sauerkraut and pickles, and wrapped in foil. During Mardi Gras season, street vendors serve hot dogs on a deep fried bun.

ALASKA

The Alaska Dog, commonly referred to as the Reindeer Hot Dog, is made from caribou meat. Split, grilled and served on a steamed bun, the flavor is similar to venison sausage, albeit slightly less gamey. Typical condiments include grilled onions de-glazed with Coca-Cola, mustard, and cream cheese a la Seattle-style. Reindeer links are smoked, natural-casing dogs blended with a mix of caribou and beef seasoned with coriander. Nota bene: Reindeer meat is too lean to hold together without beef fat being added.

ARIZONA

Popular in **Tucson** and elsewhere in southern Arizona, as well as across the border in Mexico, the Sonoran Hot Dog originated in Hermosillo, the capital of Sonora. This Southwestern favorite is wrapped in a slice of mesquite-smoked bacon, heated on either a grill, a griddle or a comal, then placed on a *bolillo* roll, or a slice of white bread, and topped with a basic load of pinto beans, grilled onions, green peppers, chopped fresh tomatoes, mayonnaise, mustard and jalapeño salsa or sauce, and finally shredded yellow or *cotijo* cheese. It is commonly served with a side of fresh-roasted chili pepper.

Phoenix- At the Arizona Diamondbacks' Chase Field, we

found a wide variety of hot dogs that change along with the season. Among the offerings are: The Arizona Dog, a foot-long, all-beef hot dog kicked up with chorizo sausage, nacho cheese and colorful, confetti-like tortilla strips. Thanks to the chips, this dog has crunch.

The Cheeseburger Dog is a tube of ground beef battered and deep-fried, plopped onto a hot dog bun, then dressed with chopped bacon, pickle, lettuce, green onion, cheddar cheese, tomato and a secret sauce.

While the Chile Verde Mac Dog features green chile macaroni and cheese piled on top of a hot dog.

The D-Bat Dog is an 18-inch long corn dog wrapped in bacon and stuffed with cheddar cheese and jalapeños. While the Venom Dog is a foot-long habanero sausage topped with black beans, guacamole, pico de gallo and sour cream.

The 2-foot long Boomstick is smothered in chili, Nacho cheese, jalapeños and onions.

CALIFORNIA

In **Los Angeles** Pinks' legendary Hollywood hot dog shack has been in business since 1939 with a menu that evolved with the times. Current editions include the Martha Stewart dog topped with relish, onions, bacon, chopped tomatoes, sauerkraut and sour cream.

Another creation is named for Gustavo Dudamel, the L.A. Philharmonic's current music director and conductor. Its toppings include guacamole, both American and Swiss cheese, jalapeño slices and tortilla chips.

The Downtown Dog, alternatively known as the Danger Dog, is a Mexican-style bacon-wrapped hot dog with grilled onions, jalapeños, bell peppers, mustard, ketchup and salsa as condiments. The term Danger Dog is said to derive from its cheap quality, as it is often sold by unlicensed street vendors.

The Doyer Dog derives its name from Mexican fans

pronunciation of the Dodgers, *Los Doyers*. Basically, this beef frank is piled high with nacho cheese, jalapenos, chopped tomatoes and onions. Doyer Fries are loaded up the same toppings as the Doyer Dog.

The Los Angeles Dodger Dog, also named after the Major League Baseball franchise, is a 10-inch ballpark frankfurter of a beef/pork blend served in a steamed bun. Interesting to note, there are two lines at Dodger Stadium concession stands, one for steamed and the other for grilled. Grilled Dogs are considered the classic version.

Yet another variation, the *Super* Dodger Dog is 100% beef .The venerable Brooklyn Dodger Dog, thicker but shorter, boasts an all-natural casing that snaps when bitten into. The deep red dog comes in a lightly toasted bun, dressed with ketchup, school-bus yellow mustard, relish and onions and wrapped in butcher paper.

In **Anaheim**, at the Los Angeles stadium, reigns the Halo Dog, a Mexican-style street dog, all-beef hot dog , wrapped with bacon and topped with charro beans, shredded Monterey Jack cheese and pico de gallo salsa.

Also in LA, we find the Swiss Schnauzer, a bratwurst with Swiss cheese topped with sauerkraut. Not exactly a hot dog, yet still worthy of mention.

West Hollywood's Oki Dog is two, that's right, two, hot dogs laid down on a flour tortilla, covered with chili and pastrami and wrapped up tight like a burrito. It takes its name from a hot dog variation served on the Japanese island of Okinawa.

San Diego's classic Tijuana-style hot dog is a grilled, bacon-wrapped, all-beef wiener topped with ketchup, mustard, mayo, grilled onions and peppers.

Also in San Diego, we find a Swiss-style hot dog, called the Swiener, prepared with a hot dog and Raclette cheese, onions and/or mustard, stuffed inside a hollowed-out French baguette.

San Diego Padres Sonoran Dog is hearty roll stuffed with an all-beef hot dog spiral-wrapped with a slice of bacon, then topped with a choice of pinto beans, grilled onions and peppers, tomatoes, relish, tomatillo salsa, mayo, mustard, ketchup, and cheese.

At **San Francisco** Giants AT&T Park we find the Tres Agaves Dog, a Mexican-style street-cart dog. It's a bacon-wrapped dog dressed with chipotle mayonnaise, sweet grilled onions, jalapeños and cucumber pico de gallo.

In **San Francisco** a bacon-wrapped hot dog is called a Mission dog, named after the Mission District where it is typically served with grilled onions, mustard, ketchup, mayonnaise, and jalapenos.

Also very popular in the Mission District is the Ham-and-Cheese dog, a smoked, bacon-studded frank topped with ham, cheddar-beer sauce, pickled jalapeños and chopped green onions

In **Tijuana** the Soano Suizo's Super Dog is so mammoth it's served on a wooden paddle. This big hot dog tucks into a sturdy baguette wrapped in slices of Swiss cheese and topped with tomatoes, peppers and crispy onions.

COLORADO

Served at Coors Field, home of the Colorado Rockies, the Rockie Dog is a foot-long topped with grilled peppers, sauerkraut and onions.

Also in **Denver**, Biker Jim's offers the exact opposite of a ballpark frank. Its exotic hot dogs are sausages made with custom cuts of pork and veal, elk, buffalo, duck, reindeer, pheasant, boar and rattlesnake. The franks are split, grilled till charred, then topped on a bun with Coca Cola-soaked grilled onions and a drizzle of cream cheese.

In **Avon,** the Swiss Hot Dog Company toasts a French baguette, lays on freshly chopped onions and a bit of parsley followed by two franks placed in the middle and topped with spicy mustard, clover sprouts, and a spice mix. The spice mix includes a sprinkling of coriander.

CONNECTICUT

Other than being served on New England rolls, there is no particular Connecticut style. Hot dogs are customarily served plain so customers can dress the condiments to suite their own tastes: Hot pepper relish, brown mustard or ketchup only, or loaded with sauerkraut, onions, and pickly chili. Interesting to note, hot dogs served with everything are described as up or four up.

In **Fairfield.** Rawley's is known for dual-cooked dogs, with the hot dog first dropped into a deep fryer before finishing up on a grill. In **Ridgefield,** Le Hot Dog Suisse is built with cheese fondue, horseradish sauce and chopped onions.

FLORIDA

Miami's El Cubano is a Cuban variation on the theme that tops a beef hot dog with bacon, grilled onions, ham, melted Swiss cheese and a pickle spear.

GEORGIA

In environs of **Atlanta**, and parts south, hot dogs are topped with coleslaw and sweet, sweet, Vidalia onions.

The Atlanta Braves' Dixie Dog is nothing less than a half-pound, foot-long, all beef, deli hot dog featuring flash-fried pulled barbecue pork, low-country mustard barbecue sauce (mustard -based) and Southern-style cole slaw.

Columbus - A local favorite, the Scramble Dog (pronounced, dawg and it's the Scramble, not Scrambled), is a chopped or plain, red-skinned hot dog served on a toasted white bun, covered by spiced chili, onions and pickles with a sprinkling of oyster crackers or crumbled Saltines. The chili contains beans and large chunks of diced raw onion.

In **Fitzgerald** a variation on the theme of Scramble Dog features two, sliced hot dogs on a bun served on a banana-split dish with mustard and catsup and smothered with chili, cole slaw, and sliced dill pickles and of course the prerequisite oyster crackers. Finally, it is topped it with sliced dill pickles and slaw.

A **Macon** variation is the spicy hot dog with its red casing are served with either chili or Coleslaw. This foot-long, half-n-half variation consists of the entire length of the hot dog topped with mustard. Half of the hot dog is topped with coleslaw and the other half is topped with chili.

A variation, adds chopped onion to the chili dog end, essentially what we have here is a half and half, a slaw dog on one end and a chili dog on the other.

HAWAII

Hot dogs are served in a myriad of variations on the Islands of Hawaii. Portuguese sausage (ground pork flavored with paprika and vinegar) has been a big part of the Hawaiian diet since the time of the European explorers and is served in slices with breakfast or incorporated in chili over rice.

The Puka is a pork and beef hot dog served on either a sweet, or Hawaiian, bread roll and topped with salsa made of finely chopped pineapple, red onion and cilantro. It is often wrapped in bacon. The word *Puka* means hole in Hawaiian. Special loaves are baked on a special appliance which creates a tunnel/hole for grilled a hot dogs to be jammed into the opening.

Puka dogs are dressed with any combination of secret sauces, tropical mustards and fruit relish: Think habanero, lemon, mango, coconut, papaya, guava, and the like. The standard condiment is a lemon garlic sauce similar to aioli.

Portuguese sausages called *Manapu* can, also be found baked into a sweet bun, or on a standard hot dog roll with mustard. The Waffle Dog is heated inside a waffle, made on a custom iron.

The Andagi Dog is a hot dog poked onto the end of a stick, and dipped in vanilla-laced Japanese doughnut batter and deep fried like a corn dog. Roadside shaved ice stands serve hot dogs on buns, American style, adding island flavor in the form of pineapple mustard or sweet Maui onions.

At bakeries hot dog *musubi* is a hot dog split and wrapped in seaweed with sticky rice sushi style.

IDAHO

Just off campus from the University of Idaho, located in downtown Iowa City, Ohio one finds a hot dog without a bun, but instead a wiener laid down in a baked potato split wide open and dressed liberally with bacon bits, chives and sour cream.

ILLINOIS

The **Chicago** Dog is a unique creation with a salad on top. This interplay of hot and cold, crisp and soft, sharp and smooth, has become America's original fast food and a true Chicago institution. Back in the day a hot dog cost a nickel and there were enough toppings included to make it a meal.

More particularly, a Chicago-style hot dog is a steamed Red Hot Chicago, Vienna Beef hot dog topped with sliced/diced/wedged tomatoes, both a dill pickle spear and sweet pickle relish (a particularly bright green style of relish, referred to as "nuclear green" relish), yellow mustard directly on the sausage, pickled sport peppers and finished with celery salt, and served on a steamed poppy seed bun. Chicago-style hot dogs are never dressed with ketchup, though some vendors offer small packets of the condiment for those savages wanting to add it. The nuclear green relish is also known as piccalilli.

The Vance Law Dog, named in honor of former the Chicago Cubs player, features a traditional Chicago-style hot dog topped with Cole slaw and ketchup. A simpler version is a steamed natural-casing dog with only mustard, onions, plain relish and sport peppers, wrapped up with hand-cut fries.

In Chicago a variation of the West coast Danger Dog is the Francheezie. Typically found at greasy spoon restaurants, it's a jumbo hot dog split down the middle and its split cavity filled with either Cheddar cheese or Velveeta. Wrapped in bacon and deep-fried, it's served on a toasted bun. A Macaroni and Cheese is a hot dog topped with, you guessed it, macaroni and cheese.

IOWA

The Great State of Iowa boasts a wider variety of hot dog creations than ought to be legal. Its Pigs in a Blanket are nothing more complicated than whole wieners wrapped in pastry dough (Pillsbury croissant) and baked in the oven. Some chefs get creative and add chives, garlic and other spices to the dough.

Hot dog Hors d' Oeuvres are chunks of franks skewered with a toothpick alongside a healthy-sized chunk of Velveeta Cheese.

An Iowa State Fair favorite is the venerable corn dog, affectionately known as a Carnie dog (carnival) stuck through one end with a long stick, unceremoniously dipped in cornbread batter and then deep-fried.

Eminently popular at potlucks and church picnics are hot dogs in Jell-O. Essentially, the soul of this farm-country dish is a mold of grape, orange or any other flavour of Jell-O with hot dogs (Either chopped up tiny or in rounds) in suspension along with fruit and even coleslaw.

In small town Iowa diners I've been pleasantly surprised by gourmand hot dog creations like: The Fruity Dog, a hot dog topped with a big spoonful of Newman's Own peach salsa; A Russki dressed with barbecue sauce, thin slices of red onions and a mound of grated cheddar cheese and; The Hayden Dog, a blistered, deep-Fry-ed (sic) frank served on a toasted bun topped with homemade coleslaw, cilantro-onion-lime relish, American cheese product and sesame mayo.

Believe it or not, Iowa anglers on the Mississippi River have been known to use chunks of hot dogs on treble hooks as catfish bait, but that's a subject for another book.

KANSAS

The Kansas City Dog, a first cousin to the Reuben sandwich, is topped with sauerkraut, melted Swiss cheese and served on a sesame seed bun. Point of relevant curiosity, the Reuben Sandwich, usually considered a New York invention, was actually created in Nebraska by Reuben Kolakofsky. At the Kansas City Royals' Kauffman Stadium, the All-Star BBQ Dog is an all-beef frank topped with pulled pork, tangy coleslaw and pickles, and slathered in barbecue sauce.

MAINE

The most famous hot dog in Maine is affectionately known as the Flo Dog. This otherwise ordinary hot dog is steamed, tucked into a buttered split-top bun and dressed with mayo, celery salt and Flo's molasses-brown relish. The latter is chutney-like, flavored with a sweet and spicy combination of onion and molasses. Paired with mustard, it becomes hotter. While paired with mayo, it's flavour comes off as tangy-sweet. Flo Dogs come in two basic versions: Either natural-casing, or steamed.

New Gloucester At the Bresca & the Honey Bee, a small, yellow, summer cook shack located on Outlet Beach, the Hot Dog Indochine features pickled carrot, radish, cilantro, basil, Fresno chili, cucumber, citrus chili, mayo and hoisin sauce loaded on top a beef dog.

Other variations on site include the Roman Dog replete with chicories, crouton, shaved Parmesan, lemon confit, roasted garlic dressing and anchovies. And the Deli Dog topped with shaved cabbage, apple and crispy onion slaw, citrus mayo, mustard, bagel seeds. While the Maple Leaf Dog features Maple Leaf brand Top Dogs dressed with local cheese curds, hot pickled peppers and maple onion jam

Portland is where the Blue Rooster Food Company features its Pineapple Express, a bacon-wrapped hot dog dressed with pickled mango salsa, cilantro jalapeño and pineapple mustard.

Rooster's Tokyo Drift is dressed with pickled ginger, wasabi mayonnaise, Japanese snack mix, and scallions. The Slawsky and Hutch is dressed with tangy all beef chili, Brussel sprouts, cole slaw, brown mustard, and topped with tater tots.

MARYLAND
Baltimore Orioles fans top their hot dogs with macaroni and cheese followed by a generous lump of crab meat, seasoned with Old Bay seasoning. The name of this creation is The Crab Mac & Cheese Dog. A variation on the Midwest's fried bologna sandwich can be found in Maryland by way of a thick slice of bologna wrapped around a pan-fried hot dog dressed with mustard.

MASSACHUSETTS
Boston - Fenway Park is home to the Fenway Frank. A legendary favorite of Red Sox fans, it's boiled or grilled and served on a New England style bun along with mustard and relish.

Boston Style Hot Dogs are usually served steamed, not grilled. Toppings include ketchup, mustard, relish, piccalilli, chopped onions and Boston baked beans.

At the Bronwyn restaurant, the Brondog Germanic Chili Dog features a blend of ground pork shoulder and ground beef leg, and smoked onion, slathered in sauerkraut, Emmenthaler Swiss and sauerbraten (roast brisket marinated in vinegar).

Too often the ubiquitous corn dog presents itself as a rubbery hot dog and coasted with cornmeal batter and deep-fried to the consistency of rubber. The Gallows, however, dips its beef brisket hot dogs in a moist batter similar to airy tempura.

Michael's Deli wraps its hot dogs in a heaping pile of pastrami and sauerkraut served on either a roll or rye bread.At The Butcher Shop, Hot Dog à la Maison dogs are made from ground bacon and pork, seasoned with coriander, white pepper, and various warming spices. The mixture is stuffed into a hog casing, which makes them thicker than a conventional hot dog. They are first poached, then oven roasted and finally served on a Parker House roll slathered with bread-and-butter pickled fennel.

In the early 1970s Boston's Sizzlebord was located near the downtown bus station where its Swiss style hot dogs wrapped in Swiss cheese were served on a steamed bun. Sadly, the vendor is long gone. This delight could be recreated with a grilled hot dog stuck in a steamed bun then smothered in sautéed mushrooms and either Swiss or Raclette cheese.

The Boston Strangler is a foot-long, topped with sautéed onions and Mackin' Cheese (rotini noodles, cheddar, jack cheddar cheese sauce, and crumbled Ritz crackers). It is of course served on a toasted, traditional New England hot dog bun.

In Northeastern Massachusetts hot dogs are most often boiled and served with mustard and sweet relish with, or without, a bun. When served with a bun, it's often a top-loaded bun with no crusts. These hot dogs are served most frequently with baked beans. Many Northeastern diners serve slices of brown bread with hot dogs. Prepared with, or without, raisins. Molasses-based brown bread is steamed, not baked, in a can or jar. The loaf is sliced into rounds and then slathered with generous pats of butter or margarine. Some New Englanders serve the hot dog on a plate to be cut and eaten with a fork, or cooked in with the beans.

In Southeastern Massachusetts (**Taunton, Attleboro, & Fall River**) hot dogs, differ from those served in metro Boston. Here hot dogs are slow grilled and served a la Coney Island-style, which is to say, on a steamed bun with a bean-less chili, chopped onion, mustard and celery salt.

In **Methuen** and neighboring **Lawrence** hot dogs are boiled, and dressed with fried onion mixed in with melted American cheese and served in a top-loaded bun with no crusts on the side. The hot dog is either topped with mustard or left bare. Garlic is sometimes mixed in with the fried onions.

The **Berkshires** are home to a number of shops specializing in minuscule chili dogs. For example, Jack's Hot Dog Stand, in **North Adams**, is the purveyor of teeny-tiny chili doggy. Jack's dogs are bigger than some of their truly mini Berkshires brethren,. The chili (meat no beans) is rendered down to its savory essence. The cheese is white American; the bread is squishy, common supermarket fare. Mustard and onions dress the dog.

MICHIGAN

In southeastern Michigan, restaurants serve Coney dogs. Popularized early in the 20th century by Greek immigrants, Coneys are very specific as to the ingredients: A natural-casing beef or beef and pork European-style Vienna sausage of German origin having a natural lamb or sheep casing; Topped with a beef heart-based sauce; One or two stripes of yellow mustard and diced or chopped white onions.

Do not make the common mistake of confusing a Coney Island Dog with a chili dog, which is a generic ground-beef-based chili-topped hot dog. Contrary to popular opinion, a Coney Island Dog is not a New Yorker. Instead, it derives from Michigan and features a ladleful of meaty chili sauce on top of a hot dog dressed with mustard and onion. An entire restaurant industry has developed from the hot dog called Coney Islands.

In southeastern Michigan, a Coney Island hot dog is a European-style Frankfurter Würstel (Vienna sausage) of German origin with a natural lamb or sheep casing, topped with a beef heart-based sauce.

Moreover, there are three variations of Coney dog, namely:

Detroit-style
Flint-style
Jackson-style

Detroit-style, dating back to 1917, boasts a sloppy, wet chili (meaning more liquid) prepared with a soupy beef heart-based sauce.

Flint style is characterized by a dry hot dog topping made with a base of ground beef heart, ground to the consistency of fine ground beef. Truth be told it's more of a mild, hot dog topping than it is a sauce.

Jackson-style, dating back to 1914, originally featured ground beef sauce prior to switching to ground beef heart in the early 1940s. Today's Jackson style uses a topping of either ground beef or ground beef heart, onions and spices. The thick and hearty, sauce is ladled onto a quality hot dog set in a steamed bun and topped with either diced or chopped onions and dressed by a brilliant yellow stripe of mustard.

Detroit's Comerica Park, proffers the Poutine Dog. For those few souls who are unfamiliar with the concept, Poutine is nothing less than French fries topped with cheese curds and gravy. In Detroit the ballpark tops a hot dog with it.

Found mostly in southern counties of Michigan, the Mush Puppy, no relation to the Coney Dog, is a beef hot dog on a steamed cheddar hot dog bun (deep yellow in color) with melted cheddar sauce and cooked mushroom slices.

MINNESOTA
Minneapolis' The Wienery diner serves natural-casing Vienna beef franks on poppy seed buns. Toppings range from classic Chicago-style to the Upsetter, replete with bacon, cheese and topped with an egg cooked to order.

NEW JERSEY
The state of New Jersey has no single style of hot dog: Purveyors serve skinless pork-and-beef franks as well as kosher natural-casing beef. The Potato Dog features diced and stewed potatoes combined with brown mustard and served on spicy, hot dog.

In **Clifton** Rutt's Hute deep-fries hot dogs in oil. Order any one of three ways: An In and Outer (minimally warmed by the oil); The Ripper (cooked until the skin bursts); and the Cremator deep-fried to the point where the sausages burst wide open, resulting in a dense, caramelized outer casing. Rutt's rippers are dressed with homemade house relish, a blend of mustard, onions, carrots and cabbage.

Build a traditional **Newark** Style Dog by cutting a round pizza bread in half (for a double) or into quarters (for a single) and cutting a pocket into it and liberally spreading mustard all around inside. Stuff a deep-fried dog into the pocket, top with fried or sautéed onions and peppers and topped with crisp-fried potato chunks. A quicker version, called a double dog substitutes French fries for potato rounds and in some spots a Portuguese or sub roll replaces the traditional round bread.

A variant found in Jersey City features a ladleful of chili, finely minced onions with a red chili-flavored sauce but no meat.

In Lafayette the Bull Dog, comes replete with a deep-fried, ¼ pound hot dog served on a sub roll along with white American cheese, relish and crisp bacon.

The Italian hot dog, served in and around Newark, is a quarter round slightly crusty Italian bread was filled with skinless beef hot dogs and grilled or sautéed peppers and onions, then topped by fried potato rounds.

The Texas Hot Dog was created in Paterson, New Jersey sometime before 1920. Texas refers to the chili sauce and the hot dog proper can be either grilled or deep-fried topped served with spicy brown mustard, chopped onions and a meat sauce somewhat similar to chili.

Similarly, John's Texas Weiners (sic) in Newark either grills or deep fries hot dogs then tops with spicy brown mustard, chopped onions and a meat sauce similar to chili. Order all three condiments as: All the Way means dressed with Düsseldorf mustard (as opposed to the Coney, which uses yellow mustard), diced onions, and chili sauce.

34

In New Jersey and elsewhere up and down the East Coast, the Jersey Breakfast Dog is a bacon-wrapped, deep-fried hot dog with melted cheese, laid down on top of either a fried or scrambled egg.

NEW YORK STATE

A Big Apple hot dog comes dressed with steamed onions or sauerkraut and dressed with a pale, deli-style yellow mustard. In upstate New York State red hots and white hots are popular fare. Red hots are normal hot dogs.

The white hot, or porker, as it has affectionately come to be known, combines uncured and un-smoked pork, beef, and veal. White hots are plumper, similar to a German Bockwurst and often natural casing. White hots are almost exclusively dressed with spicy brown mustard.

A Red Hot variant served throughout the Adirondacks is cased in a red-dyed natural-sheep-casing. Known as a Glazier it's typically offered as an alternative to a regular hot dog, usually for a small additional charge.

Michigans are hot dogs with a meaty sauce , with a texture more like a Sloppy Joe than chili (no chili-oregano-cumin). The Michigan is served in a buttered-grilled Frankfurt loaf (a bun with no crust on the sides).

The Capital District (**Albany, Troy, Schenectady**) is a happy home to a small hot dog measuring a scant 3-inches in length and served with mustard, onions, and a spicy, meat sauce.

Buffalo, Rochester and **Western New York** state are known for charcoal-broiled hot dogs cooked over hardwood charcoal.

Buffalo, famous for Buffalo chicken wings, wraps a wiener in a strip of apple wood-smoked bacon and appropriately tops it off with Buffalo mustard and crumbled blue cheese.

Kingston is the home to Dallas Hot Wieners franchises that serves a steamed skinless hot dog topped with its proprietary Dallas Wiener Sauce, made with meat, finely-chopped onions and mustard.

Heidi's in **Liverpool,** famous for qualifying as one of the oldest drive-ins in the country griddle fries its white Coney (made with pork, veal and egg whites) served either one or two franks on a New England-style split-top roll. Heidi's only allows mustard topping for its flat-grilled sausages.

Mamaroneck Walter's uses the same unique combination of ingredients that Walter Warrington originated in 1919, namely pork, beef, and veal (no casing).

It is cooked on the grill, split down the middle, browned and served on toasted rolls with either Walter's own brown mustard relish mix, plain brown mustard or (Gasp!) ketchup.

New York City - You already know hot dogs are readily available at the army of carts on street corners as well as inside delicatessens and at ball parks. Yankee Stadium boasts boiled Nathan's Famous hot dog (a water dog), a classic all-beef natural-casing hot dog served on a steamed bun.

Citi Field concession stands showcase flat-top Vienna all-beef or chicken, apple, and sage sausage dogs, split and griddled until crispy on the outside.

The **Brooklyn Diners'** snappy all-beef hot dog weighs almost a pound, a 15-bite hot dog if there ever was one. It comes with onion rings and sauerkraut studded with juniper berries.

Manhattan's Serendipity 3 Restaurant's Haute Dog is literally a Guinness World record holder. Haute Dog is a foot-long, grilled in white truffle oil, and served on a homemade pretzel-style bun brushed with truffle butter before being topped with duck foie gras, caramelized Vidalia onions, black truffle Dijon mustard and homemade heirloom tomato ketchup. Its price, and hence Guinness notoriety, is a lofty $69. Take a deep breath, Serendipity 3 Restaurant's daily-fare foot-longs only cost $8.50 replete with chili and chopped onions cheddar cheese bacon and cheddar cheese.

At Madison Square Park, Danny Meyer's hot dog stand offers

a Vienna all-beef dog split down the middle, griddled crisp and either dressed Chicago-style, or Dapper which is to say topped with cheddar and American cheese sauce and ale-marinated shallots.

NORTH CAROLINA

North Carolinian hot dogs boast a distinctive red color and are prepared Carolina-style which includes chili, coleslaw and onions. Mustard sometimes replaces coleslaw, or can be added as a fourth condiment. For those whose taste buds find the flavor of sauerkraut too sour, a slaw dog may be a welcome alternative. North Carolina, hot dogs topped with chili, onions, and either mustard or slaw are referred to as Carolina style, which is also used to refer to hamburgers with similar toppings. Both North Carolina and South Carolina hot dogs are served with chili and Cole slaw, mustard, and onions. While most vendors use coleslaw, some establishments dress with a vinegar-based variation called BBQ slaw, an eastern North Carolina variant called All the Way and/or a Slaw Dog. In North Carolina, a cheese dog is made with a hot dog-sized chunk of American cheese in place of the sausage; a hot dog with both sausage and cheese is called a combination dog, and a dee-luxe dog adds bacon.

NORTH DAKOTA

In Grand Forks, and other locations in the state, Red Pepper taco chain offers the Coney Dogg (sic: spelled with two 'g's), relatively large at 4.0 ounces topped with Mexi-meat which, unlike most Coney Island toppings, is a thick and mildly-sweet Mexican chili. Coney Dogg is topped with a pile of finely-shredded Colby cheese.

OHIO

In greater **Cincinnati**, Cheese Coneys or Coney Islands (without the cheese) are a hot dog topped with Cincinnati chili (a

Greek-inspired meat sauce), mustard, diced onion and shredded, mild cheddar cheese.

At Cincinnati Reds stadium Cheese Coney get a ladleful of Skyline saucy chili with (barest hints of cinnamon and chocolate), topped with chopped onions and a heaping helping of shredded, Cheddar cheese.

Cleveland's Polish Boy can be either a kielbasa or a hot dog, either grilled or fried, then served on a bun layered with French fries and sweet, Southern-style barbecue sauce slathered on top, or in the alternative, hot sauce and a layer of coleslaw. At Indians' baseball games, and elsewhere in the environs, hot dogs are topped with Stadium Mustard, similar in flavor and colour to Dijon mustard. At Progressive Field, home of the Cleveland Indians, the Slider Dog is topped with macaroni and cheese, a pile of chopped bacon and colourful sprinkling of Froot Loops.

Columbus is where Dirty Franks serves Vienna all-beef wieners with more than 20 topping to choose from, including like brisket, corn relish and Sriracha-cream cheese.

Toledo Tony Packo's Cafe (immortalized in an episode of the TV series M.A.S.H.) serves a Hungarian sausage about twice the thickness of a conventional hot dog, sliced in half before grilling and topped with the restaurant's proprietary spicy chili sauce.

OKLAHOMA
Oklahoma Coneys are small hot dogs served on steamed buns with a ladleful of spicy-sweet, dark brown chili sauce, onions, cheese and hot sauce.

Tulsa is the proud home of the Coney I-Lander, a miniature chili dog measuring ¾ of an inch thick by nine-inches long. Their slightly spicy chili topping is mix of beef and flour. These slow-grilled hot dog dressed with mustard and finely shredded medium sharp cheddar cheese sit pretty in a steamed bun. These coneys are much smaller than a typical hot dog.

PENNSYLVANIA

Two common variants in the Allentown, Bethlehem and Easton metro areas include the Valley Chili Dog, a grilled dog served on a steamed roll with chili 'meat sauce,' mustard, and onions and often served with deep fried pirogues instead of the traditional side dish of French fries.

A second variant, called a Mop Dog, is a shallow fried dog served on a steamed roll dressed with mustard, chopped white onion, and a dill pickle spear.

In **Philadelphia**, street vendors sell hot dogs topped with one or more of several traditional Philadelphia condiments: Ketchup, mustard (ball park yellow and/or spicy brown), chopped onions (cooked/soft or raw), relish, and (without exception) sauerkraut.

Philadelphia boasts several variety of intriguing hot dog recipes. Phillies Citizens Bank Park's signature item is the Chicago Dog, a classic ballpark treat done up Windy City style, which means topped with sweet green relish, hot peppers, and diced onions and tomatoes and served on a poppy seed bun.

At Phillies Stadium the signature item is the Chicago Dog, a classic ballpark treat done up Windy City style, topped with sweet green relish, hot peppers, and diced onions and tomatoes, and all served on a poppy seed bun.

The Texas Tommy, popular in Philadelphia and elsewhere in Eastern Pennsylvania, is quite similar to a francheezie: A split hot dog filled with cheese then wrapped in bacon. Texas Tommy comes either deep-fried, broiled, or grilled.

The classic Philadelphia Dog features an all-beef hot dog sharing the bun with a fish cake, the combo is dressed with a sweet vinegary slaw and spicy mustard.

At Pittsburg Pirates Stadium (PNC Park), the Smokehouse Dog is foot-long, all-beef dog covered in crispy fried onions, as well as some extra meat in the form of pulled-pork flavored with Kansas City-style barbecue sauce.

Also at PNC Park the Cracker Jack & Mac Dog is topped with

macaroni and cheese and Cracker Jacks, along with some caramel sauce and jalapeños.

There too resides the **Pittsburgh** Dog, an 18-inch hot dog served on a hoagie roll along with shredded lettuce, diced tomato, dry Cole slaw and strips of Provolone cheese.

At Station Street hot dogs are all beef with natural casings. Toppings range from Po' Boy (fried oysters, lettuce, tomato, pickles, mayo, mustard) to the *banh mi* (pork liver, pickled cucumber, pickled red onion, jalapeño , sweet chili and cilantro)

RHODE ISLAND

The New York System hot dog is typically made from a small, thin, hot dog made of veal and pork, lending it a different flavour than a traditional, beef hot dog. Served on a steamed bun, the hot dog is topped with a meat sauce seasoned with a myriad of spices like cumin, paprika, chili powder, and allspice, which is itself covered in finely chopped onions, celery salt, and yellow mustard. Served to go, wrapped in white paper, New York System Wieners are called gaggers (pronounced gaggas).

TENNESSEE

Memphis offers a bacon wrapped hot dog in a bun dressed with barbecue sauce, chopped scallions and shredded cheddar cheese.

TEXAS

Austin - The Jackalope is a smoked antelope, rabbit and pork sausage. Bun choices include gluten-free, pretzel or a tortilla wrap At the Texas Rangers Ball Park in **Arlington**, the Boomstick is a one-pound hot dogs topped with chili meat, sautéed onions, and cheese and sits in a two-foot-long bun.

Named after Texas Rangers pitcher, Robbie Ross, the Totally Rossome Dog is topped chili, cheese, jalapeño peppers, brisket and a handful of broken up Doritos.

At the **Houston** Astros Minute Maid Park the Cincinnati Cheese Coney is a jumbo hot dog dolled up with fiery chili and cheddar cheese, then topped with diced onion. Also at Minute Maid Park, Houston, the Texas Dog comes replete with chili, cheese and jalapeños. The stadium's Georgia Dog comes replete with coleslaw, chopped onions, and barbecue sauce. While the Ken Hoffman is a New York Dog dressed with grilled sauerkraut and spicy mustard.

VIRGINIA

Most places in Central Virginia serve grilled or lightly deep-fried hot dogs. With the quality of the sausage varies from all-meat franks to all-beef products the meaning of the terms All the Way, or Everything, can vary slightly.

That being said, condiments are universally yellow mustard, chili, and onions. Some restaurants offer coleslaw at an extra charge, while others include coleslaw as the fourth condiment. Although sweet relish is usually available, as is ketchup, these are not automatically added.

WASHINGTON, D.C.

Our Nation's Capital offers a half-smoke, which is to say a half pork, half beef sausage. It's like a hot dog only slightly larger and spicier than a conventional dog, which features coarsely ground meat and extra spice. Top a half-smoke with chili, mustard and onions.

Another DC variation is the Monumental Dog, a steamed or grilled rectangular all beef hot dog served on a steamed potato bun, with a spread of mayonnaise on the bun, topped with banana peppers, onions, tangy diced red peppers, and sliced pickles.

At Washington Nationals' Stadium, the quarter-pound, signature dog hails from a local joint, namely: Ben's Chili Bowl.The Original Chili Half Smoke is a family recipe that blends fresh, lean ground beef, ground pork and secret spices to make a half smoked dog, slathered in a rich, saucy chili, onions and cheddar cheese, also known as an All the Way.

WASHINGTON STATE

Seattle hot dogs are renowned for their unique twist: A sweet, cream cheese stuffing. The hot dogs are split in half, grilled then put in a toasted bun and topped with grilled onions. Sriracha sauce and jalapeños are popular additions as well

At the Seattle Mariner's Safeco Field, Ivar Dogs feature a slice of cod fish placed in a hot dog bun covered in coleslaw. Okay, folks, no matter what you may call it, this is not a hot dog any more than the so-called Seattle dogs featuring salmon.

A Chehalis Breakfast Dog is baked in biscuit dough wrapped with a strip of bacon. It is alternatively known as a Chehalis Pork Wellington, or when cheese is added, a Chehalis Cor-dog Bleu.

WEST VIRGINIA

West Virginia Hot dogs are served with a bean-less chili con carne made with finely ground beef (simply called chili) and sweet coleslaw or with some combination of the chili sauce, sweet creamy Coleslaw, yellow mustard and chopped onions served on a steamed bun wrapped up in parchment paper.

While the chili adds a spicy kick, the slaw balances the heat with its cool sweetness. A great West Virginia Hot Dog must have these two elements working together in the right combination. If chili isn't spicy enough a sweet slaw will dominate too much while a bland slaw would allow a spicy chili to overpower the taste buds.

In **Huntington** hot dogs are served with chili sauce. Each one of the town's numerous hot dog stands feature a slightly different variation of sauce ranging from a pinto bean-based paste to a thick pile of well-seasoned ground beef. Hot dogs with sauce are often ordered with Coleslaw, mustard, onions, cheese sauce, and/or ketchup.

As noted above, in areas where it is called sauce, the substance is usually more finely ground and more liquid in consistency. Other than that, a general rule of thumb is that the further south you travel, the less spicy the chili. The prototypical West Virginia hot dog begins with a hot dog on top of a soft steamed bun. Add mustard, a chili-like sauce and top it off with creamy coleslaw (not too sweet) and chopped onions. West Virginia has variations on the theme, but the common elements remains: Sweet, creamy coleslaw and chili. The onions vary by time of year and location. Some aficionados prefer yellow onions for their potency, while others prefer the sweetest onion available. Onions also vary from finely grated to coarsely chopped.

Unlike New Yorkers or Chicagoans, West Virginia Hot Dog aficionados are not particularly concerned with the taste of the hot dog. Truth be told, even a ho-hum wiener tastes great when chili and slaw are singing in perfect harmony.

So exactly how does a West Virginia Hot Dog differ from a Slaw Dog? The answer is as simple as the sea is salt. A slaw dog is a hot dog with slaw on it. It is usually sold as an option in hot dog joints where a standard hot dog includes only chili/sauce. Suffice it to say if you have to ask for slaw on a hot dog, it's not a true West Virginia Hot Dog.

WISCONSIN

Both traditional Chicago dogs and Danish-style hot dogs are served lakeside on Lake Geneva, No big surprise, the Chicago Dog features the original Chicago Seven litany of ingredients: yellow mustard, pickle spear, neon green Vienna Beef relish, onions, sport peppers, tomato wedges and celery salt.

Chicago Dogs come in two sizes, the Classic seven-inch long Vienna Beef dog poking out from the ends of the traditional poppy seed bun and the 1/5th pound Viking Dog, a mild version of the Vienna Beef skinless Polish. The Wisconsin-style Danish dog comes topped with yellow mustard, Vienna Beef, Düsseldorf mustard, ketchup, Danish Rémoulade sauce, onions, fried Danish onions and Danish pickled cucumbers.

"Sell the sizzle, not the hot dog."
Chicago Mickey – Hot Dog Cart Entrepreneur.

EUROPE

Many countries around the world have made the hot dog their own. Here's a sneak peek at how they do it.

AUSTRIA

In Austria the term hot dog refers to a hollowed-out baguette into which a sausage has been placed, along with condiments, as in France (see below), only sans cheese.

THE BASQUE COUNTRY (EL PAIS VASCO)

A Basque Dog, features *txistorra* (sausage) topped with *aioli piquillo mostardo* on a potato roll. Txistorra is a fast-cure sausage made of minced pork, or a mixture of minced pork and beef, and flavoured with garlic, salt, and paprika, which lends it a bright, red colour. Baked, fried, or grilled, it's thinner than traditional chorizo or sausage.

BELGIUM

In Belgium a basic hot dog is an all-beef frank served on a steamed poppy seed, a sauce of choice of sauces and dressed with onions, in either a long bun, a piece of baguette, as a kebab or plain and untouched.

CZECH REPUBLIC

Hot dogs in the Czech Republic are sold from carts in city centers and at the bus stations are steamed. Unlike the American style, they are not placed on a split bun. Rather, the top of the bun is cut off and a hole punched deep into the bun. The wiener is dressed with mustard and ketchup and inserted in the bun.

DENMARK

The Danish hot dog is a long, thin, red sausage steamed and

placed on bread either been warmed in an oven or a toaster and topped with ketchup, Danish mustard and Rémoulade followed by a sprinkling of raw and toasted onion, and a layer of pickled cucumber. A popular Danish variation on the theme is what's known as the French hot dog, essentially a baguette impaled on a spike with a sausage inserted an served with a French hot dog dressing, a sauce featuring Dijon mustard. Ketchup, mustard, remodel or French dressing is put in the cavity. For the record, the Danish hot dog is also popular in neighboring Germany and southern Sweden, especially in Malmö.

FRANCE

It should come as no big surprise to learn the French hot dog comes in a baguette instead of on a bun and is topped with melty, Gruyère cheese, mushroom ketchup and spicy, dark mustard. To prepare one, half a baguette is impaled on a hot metal stick that makes room for the sausage. Next Gruyère is melted on top.

The French Hot Dog with Ketcepes (mushroom-based catsup) sandwiches a frankfurter in a length of baguette, topped with cheese and grilled. A variation on the theme slathers *beurr blanc* with a splash of red wine on a baguettes followed by the hot dog, followed by a heaping mound of grated cheese melted for three minutes in an oven.

GERMANY

German sausages are commonly eaten on small paper plates with both mustard and ketchup and a small bun on the side. Held in the fingers, or with a perforated strip torn off the paper tray, the wieners are dipped into both condiments before taking a bite. Bread is eaten in between bites of the sausages and is also dipped into the condiments.

The most popular variant in Germany is Currywurst chunked and eaten with small throwaway wooden or plastic forks. Ketwurst, created in the German Democratic Republic (the former

East Germany) derives its name from the German words for ketchup and sausage.

To make one, a special Bockwurst, (larger than regular hot dogs) is warmed in water. A long roll is pierced by a hot metal cylinder, which creates an appropriately-sized hole. The sausage is then unceremoniously dunked in ketchup and inserted inside the roll. Interesting to note, Ketwurst was invented around 1977 when restaurants in the vicinity of the Berlin TV Tower were incapable of handling large numbers of hungry visitors. The crowds were the mother of invention. Considered the archetypal East German fast food, until German reunification, Ketwurst was rarely seen outside of the Berlin city center.

ICELAND

Iceland's national dish is *pylsur*, a hot-dog made from equal parts of ground beef, pork and Icelandic lamb, seasoned with salt, pepper and fresh thyme. Served on a plain, white bun and buried under a mound of crunchy deep-fried onions, raw onions, sweet brown mustard, ketchup and Rémoulade, it's washed down with Coca-Cola. The lamb deepens the flavor, the natural casings snap when you bite into them.

For those unfamiliar with Rémoulade, it's an aioli or mayonnaise-based sauce commonly served as an accompaniment to fish. But in Iceland and Denmark, it's a key hot dog condiment. This mayonnaise-based sauce features a blend of Dijon mustard, vinegar, chopped pickles, piccalilli, horseradish, paprika tarragon and parsley. Similar to tartar sauce, it's more yellowish, and is sometimes flavored with curry.

IRELAND

The Wild Irish venison sausage hot dog is typically dressed with pickled red cabbage, mustard aioli and watercress leaves.

NETHERLANDS

In Amsterdam hot dogs heated by hot air are served on bread rolls

ITALY

Hot Dogs served from carts in Rome are split in half, lengthwise, and served on a *panino* alongside lettuce and mustard. Split lengthwise. Customers add the condiments, typically mayonnaise, ketchup and sauerkraut. More particularly, that means curry ketchup or mayonnaise, although some aficionados prefer tomato ketchup, mustard or even apple sauce. Then there's the long, hot dog in a bun slathered in pizza sauce and grated mozzarella cheese before broiling.

NORWAY

The much beloved hot dog is a staple at birthday parties and on Norway's Constitution Day, as well char-grilled over a campfire. Cooked hot dogs are sold at gas stations, newsstands and snack-bars all across the country, and are generally the only food served at sporting events. The classic Norwegian hot dog (*pølse*)is a boiled, all-pork hot dog, either served on a plain white flour bun, or a flat potato bread called *Lompe* (or both of them together topped with ketchup and mustard. Besides the ubiquitous ketchup and mustard, popular toppings include raw or deep fried onions bits, pickle relish (pickled cucumbers) and *rekesalat* a condiment made from shrimp and mayonnaise.

Lompe is nothing more than flour dough enriched with potato. Lompe resembles Syrian bread, but is thinner, akin to a Mexican tortilla. Local variations include a waffle instead of lompe, lingonberry jam instead of ketchup, sweet mustard (Bergbys) and sweet, brown goat cheese (*brunost*).

When the grilled pølse was first introduced to Norway in the 50s by way of Denmark, it was eaten solo, without bread. Bread on the side became an accompaniment.

In **Bergen,** at the Tre Kroneren hot dog stand, there are more than 40 different kinds of hot dogs including homemade Reindeer Dog, and the Half-meter, a giant sausage measuring a foot and a half long so big it must be served in two buns laid end to end.

PORTUGAL
Portuguese hot dogs are dressed with shoestring fries, fried onions, julienned carrots, shredded cabbage, lots of cheese, three kinds of sauces along with ketchup, lettuce, mayonnaise and sometimes guacamole and ham.

SPAIN
In Spain, there is a wide variety of hot dog types, where they are also known as frankfurters and are usually baked with Viennese rolls, accompanied by melted cheese, bacon, fried onions and various sauces. The Tuga Dog comes with a fried egg laid down on top of tomato, chives and bacon.

SWEDEN
In **Stockholm** it seems as if you can't throw a brick without hitting a hot dog stand. In Sweden, hot dogs, a typical fast food, with choices ranging from the ordinary dog served with only bread, to the half special, a normal grilled hot dog whomped up with mashed potatoes and a mayonnaise-based shrimp salad The Kabanoss is served in a French bread roll (fralla in Swedish) with hot sauce, mustard and sauerkraut. Swedish Hot Dog on Flat Bread is a great floppy flour, tortilla smeared with a goodly quantity of mashed potatoes, next to either a grilled or boiled hot dog, followed by mustard, ketchup, green relish and dried dill, pink shrimp/crayfish salad all rolled up into a tight bundle.

SWITZERLAND
Hot dogs are sold from takeaways where the customer chooses between hot dog, porc (sic) and sometimes other

sausages. Most places rely on a special hot dog maker that contains a compartment for steaming the sausages and multiple heated rods used to make a hole in the bread and warm it.

The bread used for hot dogs is similar to a French baguette although not as long but still a bit longer than the sausage. After warming the bread, mustard and/or ketchup is inserted into the hole before adding the sausage. Due to the hole in the bread not going the whole way through, and the condiments being added from only one side, the last couple of bites of a hot dog tend to be dry which is why some only eat the part with sausage and throw away the left over bread.

Geneva's Hot Dog Faktory offers a tantalizing variety of hot dogs. For example its Curry Bombay combines curry bread, Swiss poultry sausage, Bombay mango ginger chutney sauce, and fried onions.

The Selfie is a Swiss pork sausage served on bread, dressed with ketchup de-glazed with orange juice, cabbage with white balsamic vinegar and old-fashioned mustard.

UNITED KINGDOM

In the UK, hot dogs are generally sold from hot dog food trucks (rather than carts) and are grilled or fried. They are usually served in a baguette style roll which is sealed at one end, with ketchup as the sauce, although many stands will offer a variety of sauces for the customer to add, such as mustard or barbecue sauce.

In the UK a hot dog is a hot dog and a saveloy is a seasoned highly seasoned pork sausage, usually bright red, and normally boiled but also available deep-fried in batter or served with pease pudding. The taste of a saveloy is similar to that of a frankfurter.

A type of hot dog almost indistinguishable from the saveloy is popular in the United States of America, particularly in Maine, where it is referred to as a red hot or as a red snapper.

CANADA

Calgary is where Tubby Dog serves up a number of unique hot dogs. Its A-Bomb, a 1/3 pound hot dog, comes topped with mustard, ketchup, mayo, bacon, potato chips and cheese. Its 1/3 pound Sumo Dog spreads Wasabi inside the bun, topped with Japanese Mayo, pickled ginger and a sprinkle of toasted sesame seeds.

Sherm's Ultimate Gripper is a bacon-wrapped 1/3 pound dog, deep fried, then served in a bun filled topped with a scoop of chili, then dressed with mustard, banana peppers, sautéed onions, bacon bits, grilled ham, a fried egg and finally nacho cheese.

Quebec

Steamies are top-loaded buns (called steamies because they're steamed instead of toasted or grilled). Typical condiments include mustard, onions, and fresh coleslaw and sometimes relish.

Montreal, Quebec

A Montreal hot dog and its bun can either be steamed or grilled. An all-dressed hot dog comes with deli mustard, sweet cucumber pickle relish, coleslaw and shredded raw onions. Here too, a steamed hot dog is called *un steame* (pronounced steem-ay).

A Michigan hot dog is topped with spaghetti sauce on a steamed bun generally topped with coleslaw, onion, mustard, relish, and occasionally paprika or chili powder.

Toronto, Ontario,

Hot dogs sold from carts in the downtown core are affectionately referred to as street meat. Sausages and buns are usually grilled. Condiments are self-serve and the litany of ingredients includes: ketchup, pickle relish, yellow mustard, corn relish, chopped onions, sliced cucumber pickles, bacon bits and sauerkraut. Mayonnaise, cheese and other condiment that would require refrigeration are forbidden by the city health regulations.

The Toronto Blue Jays' Great Canadian Dog is a foot-long topped with maple baked beans, crumbled Canadian back bacon and Canadian cheddar cheese.

The Whistle Dog, served by A & W restaurants in Canada, is a split hot dog served with processed cheese, bacon, and relish.

Legend has it that Babe Ruth once gorged on a dozen to 18 hot dogs before blacking out on a train ride in April of 1925.

LATIN AMERICA

ARGENTINA

A Latin cousin of the corn dog is the *panchuker*, a popular street food consisting of a baked sausage covered in a waffle-like batter fried in lard or vegetable oil. *Panchukeras* are devoted to making them and them alone. *Panchos* are another street food found in convenience stores (*quioscos*). Boiled, their most common toppings are potato sticks, and condiments: Ketchup, mustard, mayo or salsa golf. Panchos are served in long thin buns. Hot dogs measuring 12 inches are called *Superpanchos.*

BRAZIL

Brazilians love a good *cachorro quente*, literally the Portuguese words for hot dog. A cachorro quente starts life with either a steamed or boiled sausage plonked down inside is fold of a soft white bun. Then comes the avalanche of toppings: Tomatoes, corn, bacon bits, ground beef, mashed potatoes, quail eggs, ketchup, mustard, mayonnaise, grated cheese, fried slivers of potato and ultimately topped with mashed potatoes. This cornucopia of bun, dog and vegetable garden is served in a plastic bag, which it fills completely.

In Brazil quail eggs are commonplace so it should come as no big surprise to learn they end up on hot dogs. In fact, they are a standard dressing on the *cachorro-quente.*

In many regions across the country the hot dog is dressed in marinara sauce, various kinds of cheese including Parmesan, *requeijão, catupiry,* or cheddar. Like a Cuban pressed sandwich, the bun is sometimes pressed in a panini machine to lightly toast it and to melt the cheese.

Toda Nossa hot dogs (hot dogs plural) are split, griddled, and placed on bread smeared with tomato sauce, along with a slice of melty cheese on both sides, followed by a sprinkling of crunchy potato sticks and a handful of corn kernels. The sandwich too is pressed flat like a Cuban pressed sandwich and melted to the point where the hot dogs end up charred and smoky.

CHILE

A Chilean *completo* (Spanish for complete, or total) serves a sausage on a grinder roll and adds mashed avocado, chopped tomatoes, mayonnaise, sauerkraut, a variation of the sauce *américaine*, Chilean chili, green sauce and cheese. The frank is easily twice the size of an American hot dog. Other versions of completo include the Italiano liberally dressed with tomato and avocado mayo. It's being called the Italiano, also called the Tomate-Palta-Mayo (Tomato-Avocado-Mayo), or TPM for short), gives a nod to the colors of the Italian flag.

Tomate mayo, comes minimally dressed with only chopped tomatoes and mayonnaise, and it is also called *completo sin palta*, completo without avocado.

The *Dinámico* mixes tomatoes, avocados, mayonnaise and sauerkraut, or sauce américaine. It's also known as *la américana* (the American).

As (Ace) - This version consists of cuts of churrasco (grilled meat) instead of sausages, along with mashed avocado, tomato and mayonnaise. It's obviously a variant of the Italiano.

A lo Pobre (Poor boy) comes replete with fried onion, French fries and a fried egg.

Suffice it to say the term completo is generic for any hot dog dressed with avocado. Thusly, a completo-completo means topped with a plethora of condiments which can mean a generous slathering of mayo, chili, green sauce, sauerkraut, avocado, tomato and cheese.

COLOMBIA

Colombian hot dogs are *perros calientes* which in Spanish literally means hot dogs. Street stand *perros calientes* are dressed in ketchup, mustard, salsa rosada, mayonnaise, pineapple sauce, cheese and crumbled potato chips. As in Brazil, some vendors add a cooked quail's egg on top. A version called *perra* has most of the same toppings but is put together with chopped bacon and barbecue onions instead of a sausage.

High up in the mountains, around the environs of Bogotá, the hot dog is eaten with a great amount and variety of condiments and fixins' (sic). On a single hot dog it is typical to find crumbled potato chips, cheese, strings of ham or bacon, ketchup, mayo, mustard, pineapple sauce and chopped onion.

A variation of the traditional hot dog called *Perra Xtasis,* comes with chopped bacon (instead of sausage), cheese, crushed potato chips, yellow mustard, green mayo, salsa rosada, sweet yellow pineapple sauce and finally a square of American cheese melted on top. The bacon is minced finely, the small pieces salty and crispy. Rather wisely, these condiments are evenly distributed along the length and breadth of the hot dog so each bite has crunch from the finely crushed chips, sweetness from ketchup and pineapple, an herb element from the green sauce, melted cheese evenly distributed around the hot dog, salt and snap from the hot dog, creaminess from the pink mayo sauce, and the soft steamed bun as a base. Sometimes even bologna bits are added to the mix.

COSTA RICA

Here frankfurters are known as Hot Dogs, most commonly the sausage is boiled and simply dressed with ketchup, mayonnaise, mustard, pink sauce and cabbage or salad.

EL SALVADOR,

The wiener is known as a Hot Dog, Chéveres or Chorys and is fried, then dressed with pickled onion and jalapeño chili.

GUATEMALA

In Guatemala hot dogs are called *shucos* and hot dog vendors are *shuqueros*. Literally translated the word shuco, neither Spanish or Mayan in origin, means dirty. But when used colloquially to refer to a hot dog, it simply means hot dog. Shuco bread is light and airy. When toasted on the grill, the crust boasts a perfect crunch and the inside is warm and toasty. Shucos are cooked over a charcoal grill and dressed with Chirmo, (avocado sauce), boiled cabbage, mayonnaise, mustard, chopped onions, tomato sauce, mustard, hot sauce and an assorted choice of meats (sausage, chorizo (red sausage), salami, longaniza (white sausage) and bacon). One's choice of meats can include one, all or some on a single shuco. More on this a little later.

Chirmo, a classic Guatemalan condiment, is a tomato-based salsa comprised of toasted tomato sauce, chopped onion, cilantro and lemon. The Mayan word Chirmo means running nose. Chimichurri (cilantro, garlic, olive oil and pepper sauce) is another condiment.

Important to know, there are normal shucos, jumbo-sized and *ballena* (whale), each one named refers to the number of its meat toppings. Jumbos boast different five meats, while the ballena can have from ten to twenty. The customer chooses which particular meats he is hungry for. La *Ballena* shuco boasts red sausage (chorizo), white sausage (longaniza), salchicha (hot dog), ham, bacon, pepperoni, German ham and sausages, chicken breast, beef steak fajita strips, polish sausages

Mixtas are a hot dog rolled up inside a tortilla along with a lime-dressed Coleslaw, ripe guacamole, green chiles and spicy hot sauce. A variation of the mixta wraps a slice of bacon around the hot dog stuck inside a corn tortilla that is smeared with ripe avocado mash and further dressed with shredded lettuce, cabbage, mayonnaise and chopped onions. .

MEXICO

Throughout Mexico frankfurters are known by the same name as in the United States: Which is to say, hot dogs. However, they are also termed bulldog or jochos (pronounced hocho). The term jochos refers to top hot dogs dressed with Pico de Gallo, ketchup, mustard, mayonnaise and wrapping the sausage with bacon.

Traditional hot dog ingredients include chopped tomatoes and onions. In Sonora, unlike most of the rest of Mexico, chile is optional and is not part of the basic recipe. The onion may be either raw or roasted. Some street vendors add chopped lettuce and cabbage. Basic dressings include: mayonnaise, and ketchup.

The Sonoran-style, or Estilo Sonora, hot dog, native to **Hermosillo** is wrapped in mesquite-smoked bacon and cooked on either a grill, a griddle or a comal, then topped with beans, grilled onions, fresh onions, tomatoes, mayonnaise, cream sauce, mustard and jalapeño salsa or sauce and served on bread and often with a side fresh-roasted chili. The Sonoran bun is a bolillo roll. Mexico City's jocho, offered on street karts outside of nightclubs, is grilled and covered with melted Oaxacan cheese, Pico de Gallo, ketchup, mustard and bacon.

PERU

In Peru, hot dogs are affectionately known both as *panchos and as hot dogs.* A traditional pancho consists of a sausage inserted in a stick with sauces drizzled over the top. In **Lima** *salchipapa* is a popular street food, the name a portmanteau of the words *salchicha* (Spanish) and *papa* (Quechua): ie Sausage and potato. Salchipapas are thinly-sliced, pan-fried beef sausages and French fries, mixed with a savory coleslaw and dressed with *salsa rosada* (ketchup and mayonnaise), *crema de aceituna* (olive sauce), along with *aji* or chili peppers. Sometimes a fried egg or cheese is added on top. It can also come with tomato and lettuce, and occasionally garnished with dash of oregano.

URUGUAY

Panchos Porteños are hot dogs in bun with either a strip of bacon or ham set down alongside, with a melted a slice of mozzarella cheese melted on top.

VENEZUELA

Caracas and other major cities boast an impressive variety of hot dog styles (*perros calientes*). Arguably the most popular are wiener-style sausages served on steamed hot buns dressed with generous portions of chopped onion, pepper strips, sauerkraut, carrot shreds, French fries, corn niblets and/or ground Parmesan or shredded cheese. Condiments include ketchup, mayonnaise, mustard, *guasacaca*, garlic sauce, onion sauce, hot chili and tartar sauce. Variants offer things like grated potato chips BBQ sauce, cheese, bacon, ham slices, egg, chopped tomato, and yellow cheese.

ASIA MINOR

TURKEY

Besides conventional hot dogs, *Patsos* can be seen in Istanbul. Atypical from a conventional hot dog, a patsos is opened up wide and stuffed with French fries, then dressed with ketchup and mayonnaise. Patsos is an abbreviation of the two words: *patates* and *sosis*, which translates to potato and sausage.

"What better way to celebrate a meal than boiling, grilling or baking hot dogs."

Lew Diamond USMC
on Guadalcanal - 1943

SOUTH AFRICA

In South Africa, a variation of the hot dog is the *boerie roll*, Afrikaans's slang for farmer's roll. With this variation, a piece of *boerewors* is placed in a sliced bread roll then covered in tomato sauce (ketchup), mustard, chutney or a homemade tomato and onion and/or tomato relish.

More specifically, *boerewors*, a portmaneau of the Afrikaans words boer (farmer) and wors (sausage), is minced beef seasoned with pepper, nutmeg, coriander and cloves. By law, boerewors must contain at least 90-percent meat and always contain beef, as well as lamb, pork, or a mixture of lamb and pork. The other 10% is spices. Not more than 30% of the meat content may be fat. Moreover, Boerewors may not contain any mechanically recovered meat.

A *boerie* roll is boerewors, usually braised (grilled outdoors), but may be grilled on an electric griller. Alternatively it can be baked in an oven or fried in a pan. Pricking the sausage with a fork several times before heating yields sufficient fat for frying. Boerewors on a hot dog bun is served with a tomato, chili and onion relish.

There are numerous varieties of boerewors including: Garlic worst, *kameeldoring* (camel thorn), *Karoowors* (sausage from the Karoo region in South Africa), and *spekwors* made with extra cubed pork fat. Other ingredients include cheese and chili peppers.

Sausages are also stuffed with kudu or springbok meat, but it may not be sold as boerewors. Instead, it's named after the predominant meat content, if it contains at least 75% meat from that specific species.

Hollywood screen starlet Marlene Dietrich's favorite meal was hot dogs and champagne . . .

ASIA

CHINA

In Mainland China the variation of flavors is much different than that of an eastern Hot dog. First off, there are two types of hot dogs. The first type is usually sold warmed in ovens on street stands is called a Hot Dog. It is essentially starchy ground pork scrapings stuffed in a thin casing, dyed pink in color and approximately five inches long.

Another version wraps a hot dog in dumpling dough sprinkled with sesame seeds and then baked. Yet another variation is individually wrapped in a red or yellow plastic casing, available in many different sizes and flavors It has a very mild base flavor, with the texture and taste similar to that of Vienna Sausages. The most noticeable difference is the fact Chinese hot dogs are significantly less salty than their western counterparts.

HONG KONG

In Hong Kong, the Sausage Bun is a Chinese pastry made with frankfurters. Another type of hot dog found in Central Hong Kong offers the option of either one or two wieners (imported from the Netherlands) in a sweet and creamy mayonnaise covered bun. It is never dressed with mustard or with ketchup.

JAPAN

In Japan, hot dogs are sliced longitudinally in order to splay them out to resemble the eight arms of an octopus. More conventional hot dogs are also available on a stick (with or without breading), or on a bun. Curious to note, Japanese Fusion Dogs, not actually from Japan, are a Pacific Northwest (U.S.A) invention that pairs hot dogs with Japanese and Asian condiments like wasabi, kimchi and teriyaki.

KAZAKHSTAN

In Kazakhstan, hot dog-like sausages are made from horse meat stuffed in natural-casing horse intestine. The sausages can be served on bread, and are often accompanied by onion.

PHILIPPINES

Interesting to note, in the Philippines hot dogs are referred to as hotdogs (sic), spelled in just one word without the space. Hotdogs range from cocktail-sized to foot-long. Red-colored hotdogs are commonly fried and eaten with rice, as sandwiches or skewered on sticks.

Hotdogs are typically served during breakfast as street food, skewered and grilled over coals. Skewered waffle hotdogs are coated in hotcake batter and deep-fried.

Chopped hotdogs are an ingredient in Philippine-style Spaghetti Bolognesa and they pull duty as a filling in an *embutido*, sliced pieces of meat in tomato-based entrée such as *caldereta* (goat meat stew) or *menudo.*

Filipinos, unlike Chicagoans, dress dogs with ketchup. North of Manilla, notched hotdogs are served with banana, ketchup, rice and fried egg without a bun.

SOUTH KOREA

In Korea, the word for hot dog usually refers to corn dogs although American-style franks are also popular. No big surprise, given the local food culture, Kimchi is a common topping. A popular South Korean hot dog, sold at street stalls, fairs, and some fast-food restaurants, impales the frank on a stick dipped in batter before deep frying, and sometimes includes French fries in the batter.

While they may well look like corn dogs, they are instead battered, panko-crusted hot dogs. Already fried, the whole thing is tossed into an oil-filled wok for a minute or two, just to reheat and re-crisp. Upon taking a big bite, the thin layer of panko crunch yields to a softer dough layer revealing the juicy hot dog. The condiment of choice for this salty, crunchy, greasy dog is ketchup and occasionally mustard. Hot dogs on a bun or wrapped in bread are also widely available, or flying solo on a stick without any bun.

TAIWAN

Taiwanese hot dogs are either laid down onto a bun or unceremoniously poked onto the end of a stick. In night markets, meat sausages are sometimes wrapped with an outer sticky rice sausage in a snack called Small Sausage in Large Sausage. To better understand the concept, think hot dog Turduken.

THAILAND

Hot dogs are very popular in Thailand and are sold inside a bun just like an American hot dog, except instead of tomato ketchup, they're dressed with a sweet tomato-chili sauce. Street vendors deep-fry or charcoal grill hot dogs dressed with either a sweet, slightly spicy sauce (*nam chim wan*) or a very spicy sauce (*nam chim phet*). Hot dogs can either fill a croissant dressed with mayonnaise or be used as a filling for raisin bread together with shredded dried pork.

Thai Waffle hot dogs are corn dogs, only sweeter tasting and boasting a softer texture. To make them, street vendors skewer a hot dog, dunk it in waffle batter, then heat it in a waffle, hot-dog press. Once done, it is drizzled with mayonnaise, ketchup, or sweet chili sauce.

Thai Khanom Tokiao means Tokyo cake, an appellation which makes perfect sense when considering the fact that it's made from a Thai-style crepe wrapped around a hot dog dressed with sweet chili sauce.

Khao pad American translates as American fried rice, and is an American style hot dog notched with an X at both ends before heating to make it blossom when fried. Dressed with very sweet fried rice, fried chicken, ham, and raisins it is topped with a fried egg. This culinary delight dates back to the Vietnam police action of the 60's and 70's when legions of American soldiers took R&Rs in Thailand. *Donut sai krok* is the Thai name for a sausage-filled savory donut shaped like a log.

VIETNAM

Here we find a long sausage in a French roll dressed with julienned, pickled vegetables.

AUSTRALIA

In Australia, the term hot dog refers to the combination of a frankfurter and a bun dressed with ketchup and mustard. Additional toppings can include fried onions or shredded cheese. Artificial-cased frankfurters are widely available while skinless types are sometimes sold as American style.

One variation, the Dagwood Dog is hot dog poked onto the end of a stick and then covered in either wheat-based or corn-based batter then deep fried and dunked in ketchup. The wheat flour-based batter is the same recipe used for fish and chips. In other words, a Dagwood Dog is basically a corn dog. Depending on the region, it is alternatively known as a Pluto Pup, Battered Sav or the Dippy Dog,

Australia's Sausage Sizzle is a barbecued sausage on a slice of bread, topped with a condiment and/or cooked onion. Some outlets, mainly those that also serve pie floaters, serve frankfurter hot dog sandwiches with toppings including mushy peas or mashed potato.

Saveloys, popular in New Zealand and Australia, are colloquially known as savs. Consumed at fairgrounds and sporting events, savs are served on a slice of bread or in a bread roll and liberally covered in tomato sauce. Down under saveloys, are larger than the English type. Beef and chicken varieties are available at fish-and-chips shops, as in England, they are also commonly bought at butchers' shops or supermarkets to be cooked at home.

NEW ZEALAND

In New Zealand the term hot dog refers to a battered, pre-cooked sausage on a stick which has been deep fried. Similar to corn dogs, the batter is generally wheat. Usually it is served with tomato sauce or ketchup. A mere hot dog on a bun is known as an American hot dog.

RECIPES

"Hot dogs are hot dogs, hamburgers are hamburgers, sandwiches are sandwiches."

Frank Furter

BOSTON TERRIERS

Ingredients
1 white onion, diced
3 slices bacon, chopped
1 cup white beans
½ cup ketchup
½ cup water
1 Tablespoon brown sugar
1 Tablespoon mustard
1 Tablespoon cider vinegar
4 to 6 all-beef hot dogs
4 to 6 potato-style hot dog buns

Directions
Sautée onion with chopped bacon until cooked.
Mix in beans, ketchup, water, brown sugar, mustard and vinegar.
Add hot dogs and simmer until thickened, about 15 to 20 minutes.
Serve alongside hot dogs on toasted buns.

HOT DOGS IN JELL-O

Ingredients
1 small box of grape-flavored Jell-O
3 hot dogs

Directions
Warm three hot dogs in boiling water.
Remove dogs and chop into quarter-inch to one-inch long rounds.
Add grape Jell-o mix to 1 cup boiling hot dog water.
Stir the Jell-O until dissolved.
Add 2 cups ice hot cold water
Add the chopped up dogs.
Refrigerate until set.
Serve potato salad over hot dog on bun

COCA-COLA CARAMELIZED ONIONS

Ingredients
2 Tablespoons Lightly Salted Butter
2 Tablespoons Canola Oil
4 whole Large Vidalia White Onions, Sliced Thinly
1 Teaspoon Kosher or Sea Salt
1-¼ Teaspoon Black Pepper
1 Teaspoon Cumin
1 can Coca-Cola (12 ounces)

Directions
Add butter and oil to a 12-inch skillet.
Heat on medium high heat.
Once melted, add the sliced onions.
Stir and add salt, pepper and cumin.
Cook for 20 minutes.
Stir often.
The onions will transform into a nice brown color.
Once the onions are soft and translucent, drain the excess oil.
Add Coca Cola just sufficient to cover the onions.
Watch as it de-glazes the skillet and adds to its flavor.
Continue slowly cooking-off the rest of the Coke Cola.
Stir until the onions are caramelized.
When most of the liquid has evaporated, lower the heat so the onions don't burn.

HOT DOG SLAW

Ingredients
12 ½ lbs. cabbage
1 pint Yellow vinegar
3 ¾ lbs. sugar
½ gal. (64 oz.) mustard
3 red peppers, crushed
1 qt. water
6 oz. salt
1 oz. black pepper
1 lb. onion

Directions
Grate cabbage and onions.
Mix all the ingredients together.
Let stand in stone jar, covered with cheese cloth for three days.
Add enough water to almost cover.
Drain in colander.
Pack in airtight, sterile jars.

Nota bene: To grate cabbage, fill blender with about 3 ¾ cups of cabbage.

MARMET FAMOUS YELLOW SLAW

Ingredients
1 three-pound head of cabbage, shredded fine and drained
3/4 cup sugar
¼ cup honey
½ cup plus 1 Tablespoon apple cider vinegar
¼ cup plus 2 Tablespoons yellow mustard
½ Teaspoon salt
1 Teaspoon white pepper

Directions
As simple as the sea is salt, combine the ingredients in a big bowl and leave overnight in refrigerator.
Its yellow colour is from the mustard, so if the flavor is too mustardy-strong, then thin with mayonnaise.

Nota bene: This is a close approximation of the recipe from the now defunct Canary Cottage diner located in Marmet, West Virginia.

TEXAS YELLOW COLD SLAW

Ingredients

¼ cup cider vinegar
2 tablespoons dark brown sugar
½ Teaspoon celery seed
½ Teaspoon ground turmeric
¼ Teaspoon ground ginger
Pinch of ground allspice
1 small onion, finely diced
½ small head cabbage, coarsely chopped
2 Kirby cucumbers, peeled, seeded and diced
½ green bell pepper, coarsely chopped
3 tablespoons olive oil
Salt and pepper

Directions

Bring vinegar, brown sugar, celery seed, turmeric, ginger, and allspice to a boil over medium-high heat.
Stir in onions.
Remove from the heat.
Allow to stand five minutes in order to cool.
Toss the cabbage, cucumber and bell pepper together.
Whisk olive oil into the cooled vinegar mixture until combined.
Pour the onion-turmeric vinaigrette over the top of the vegetables.
Toss to coat.
Season, to taste, with salt and pepper.

WEST VIRGINIA HOT DOG CHILI

Ingredients
½ cup shortening
2 Tablespoon onions, chopped
2 cloves garlic, chopped
5 lbs. ground beef
1 ½ Tablespoon paprika
2 ½ Tablespoon chili powder
1 ½ Tablespoon black pepper
½ - 1 Tablespoon cayenne pepper
2 Tablespoon salt
2 ½ Tablespoon ground cumin
1 Teaspoon ground cinnamon
½ - 1 cup cracker meal

Directions
Sauté meat, garlic and onions until browned.
Add spices, stir well.
Add a quart of water.
Cook over low heat for three to four hours.
Occasionally add water to keep from sticking.
When the chili is cooked, remove from heat and add ½ to 1 cup of
cracker meal and stir well.

BOSTON BROWN BREAD

Ingredients
½ cup cornmeal
½ cup whole wheat flour
½ cup rye flour
½ Teaspoon baking powder
½ Teaspoon baking soda
¼ Teaspoon salt
1 cup buttermilk
1/3 cup molasses
2 tablespoons brown sugar
1 Tablespoon canola oil
3 tablespoons chopped walnuts, toasted
3 tablespoons raisins

Directions
In a large bowl, combine the first six ingredients.
In a separate bowl, whisk buttermilk, molasses, brown sugar & oil.
Stir into dry ingredients just until moistened.
Fold in the walnuts and raisins.
Transfer the mix to a greased 8- x 4-in. loaf pan.
Tent with aluminum foil.
Place pan on a rack in a boiling-water canner or other large, deep pot.
Add one inch of hot water to pot.
Bring to a gentle boil.
Cover.
Steam for 45 to 50 minutes until a toothpick comes out clean.
Add water to the pot as it evaporates.
Remove pan from the pot.
Let stand 10 minutes before removing bread from pan to a wire rack.
Serve slathered in sweet cream butter or cream cheese.

RÉMOULADE

Ingredients
Makes 1 cup
1 small shallot, finely chopped
1 scallion, finely chopped
1 Tablespoon Dijon mustard
1 Teaspoon lemon juice
1 Teaspoon tomato paste
½ cup mayonnaise
½ cup chopped dill pickle
½ Teaspoon chopped fresh oregano
½ Teaspoon chopped fresh thyme
½ Teaspoon chopped garlic
¼ Teaspoon freshly ground black pepper
⅛ Teaspoon cayenne pepper
⅛ Teaspoon paprika
Kosher salt

Directions
Whisk all ingredients together in a small bowl until smooth.
Cover and chill.

Rémoulade can be prepared up to two days ahead of time.

Nota Bene: Rémoulade is a flavorful and more colorful substitute
for traditional tartar sauce.

UTAH FRY SAUCE

Ingredients

1 cup mayonnaise

½ cup ketchup

½ tsp. onion powder

½ tsp. white vinegar (white vinegar makes it smooth and adds flavor)

3 to 4 teaspoons pickle juice (add one Teaspoon or so at a time & check for taste)

Directions

Mix together in small bowl.

Variations on the theme:

Substitute barbecue sauce or chili sauce for the ketchup.

Add kick with a dash of cayenne pepper or Tabasco sauce.

Add grated horseradish by taste.

Option

Add 1 tsp. chopped pickle relish, but know that adding pickle relish makes the concoction into Thousand Island dressing and it's no longer Utah Fry Sauce.

Nota bene: The ratio is two parts mayonnaise to one part ketchup.

HAWAIIAN SALSA

Ingredients

1 cup cut-up mango
6 sweet peppers in assorted colors, cut into large pieces
½ red onion, cut into large pieces
¼ pineapple, cut into large pieces
¼ cup canola oil
Kosher salt and black pepper
¼ cup chopped fresh Italian parsley
2 teaspoons thinly sliced green onions
1 Teaspoon honey
½ Teaspoon Cajun seasoning
10 King's Hawaiian Hot Dog Buns
10 Hot dogs

Directions for the Hawaiian salsa:
Warm a grill to medium-high heat.
Place mango, sweet peppers, red onion & pineapple in a large bowl.
Toss with the oil and season with salt and pepper to taste.
Grill fruits & vegetables until they begin to char: (3 mins per side).
Allow to cool slightly
Cut mango, peppers, red onion and pineapple into ½-inch cubes.
Add to a large bowl along with the Italian parsley, green onions, honey and Cajun seasoning.
Toss to combine, and set aside.

Nota bene: When fruit isn't quite ripe, grilling enhances its sweetness.

GUASACACA

Ingredients

1 medium onion, roughly chopped

2 green bell peppers, seeded de-veined and roughly chopped

3 ripe avocados, peeled and seeded

2 large garlic cloves

1/2 bunch fresh flat leaf parsley

1/2 bunch fresh cilantro

1/3 cup red wine vinegar

1 Tablespoon kosher salt, to taste

1/4 Teaspoon black pepper

1 cup olive oil

For dip

2 red bell peppers (optional)

2 ripe plum tomatoes (optional) or 2 Roma tomatoes (optional)

Directions

Combine everything except olive oil in a food processor.

Process until mostly smooth.

Continue processing, adding olive oil until smooth.

Scrape into a serving bowl

Let stand at room temperature one hour to allow flavors to blend.

Store in refrigerator, but bring to room temperature before serving.

CHIRMOL

Ingredients
1 big ripe juicy tomato, or two medium, or three small.
About 2 tablespoons of finely chopped white onion.
1 Tablespoon of finely chopped cilantro.
A sprinkling of chopped fresh chile.
1/4 of a lime.
1 Tablespoon olive oil.
Salt

Directions
Grill onions and tomatoes till soft.
Remove the skin of the tomatoes (blackened is OK)
Puree in blender or smash together in a bowl the tomatoes, onions, and garlic.
Add olive oil, cilantro, lime juice and salt and pepper to taste.

Note bene: Chirmol flavor is all about balance, so taste to measure whether or not sour, spicy and savory are in balance. Add lime juice, salt or chile to harmonize the flavor.

TZATZIKI SAUCE

Ingredients
2 containers Whole milk yogurt (8 ounces)
2 cucumbers - peeled, seeded and diced
2 tablespoons olive oil
½ lemon, juiced
salt and pepper to taste
1 Tablespoon chopped fresh dill
(Consider substituting mint leaves for dill for a slightly different flavor)
3 cloves garlic, peeled

Directions
Combine all of the ingredients.
Food process, blend or whisk until well-combined.
Transfer to a separate dish.
Cover and refrigerate for at least one hour.
Garnish with a sprig of fresh dill just before serving

Nota bene: Substitute half of the yogurt with sour cream for a less tangy flavour. Also, before adding the cucumber, consider letting the yogurt mixture sit overnight so the garlic gives up its sharpness. Placing the diced cucumber in a colander overnight also allows liquid to drain so the tzatziki isn't quite so watery.

MAPLE AND ONION JAM

Ingredients
¼ cups Olive Oil
8 cups Sweet Onion, Quartered and Sliced Thin
2 teaspoons Kosher Salt
1 Tablespoon Thyme
1 Teaspoon Black Pepper
1 cup Maple Syrup
¼ cups Cider Vinegar
5 four-ounce canning jars lids and rings sterilized

Directions
In an eight-inch skillet heat the olive oil and add the onions.
Cook over medium heat 10 minutes or until onions translucent.
Reduce heat to medium low.
Add salt, thyme and pepper.
Cover the skillet and cook for another 10 minutes.
Increase heat to medium and add maple syrup.
Bring to a boil and lower heat to keep simmering.
Cook uncovered another 15 minutes.
Remove the skillet from the heat and add the vinegar.
Ladle the mixture into hot sterilized canning jars
Wipe the jar rims with a damp clean towel and adjust the lids.
Process in a water bath for 10 minutes.
Remove from the water bath and cool.
Wait for the reassuring ping of the lid when it seals.

Nota bene: This recipe yields about five, 4-ounce jars.

LOW-COUNTRY BARBECUE SAUCE
(Mustard Based)

Ingredients

4 Tablespoon butter

½ sweet onion, grated

½ cup yellow ballpark mustard

½ cup brown sugar

½ cup cider vinegar

1 Tablespoon dry mustard (like Colman's)

1 Teaspoon cayenne pepper.

1 bay leaf

Salt to taste

Directions

Heat the butter over medium heat until it's frothy.

Add the onion.

Sauté for three to four minutes.

Do not let the onions turn brown.

Add the balance of the ingredients.

Stir well.

All the while simmering, for at least 30 minutes

LOW-COUNTRY BARBECUE SAUCE
(MUSTARD BASED) #2

Ingredients
1 Tablespoon garlic, minced
1/3 cup green bell pepper, chopped
3/4 cup Vidalia onion, finely diced
1 Tablespoon vegetable oil
1/2 Tablespoon crushed red pepper flakes
1/4 cup dark brown sugar
1/4 cup light brown sugar
1 Tablespoon honey
1 Tablespoon molasses
1/4 cup apple cider vinegar
2 cups prepared yellow mustard
1/4 cup ketchup
1/2 Tablespoon Worcestershire sauce
1/4 cup water
1 Tablespoon salt
1/2 Tablespoon black pepper

Directions
Sweat the garlic, green bell pepper, and onions in the vegetable oil over medium heat, until tender.
Add the crushed red pepper.
Add the brown sugar, honey and molasses.
Caramelize the mixture.
Add the vinegar
Simmer for about 15 minutes.
Add mustard, ketchup, Worcestershire, water, salt, and pepper
Simmer until reduced by one-fourth.

CHARRO BEANS

Ingredients
½ pound bacon strips
Bacon Sliced
½ cup bacon drippings
1 large onion, finely chopped
Onions Yellow/Brown
½ pound cooked h
¼ pound chorizo sausage, crumbled
5 cans pinto beans (16 ounces), rinsed and drained
1 whole chipotle pepper
2 cloves garlic, pricked with a fork

Directions
Fry the bacon strips in a large skillet over medium heat until crispy.
Transfer the bacon to paper towels in order to drain excess grease.
Reserve ½ cup bacon drippings.
Place drippings in a large pot.
Warm over medium heat.
Fry the onions until light brown.
Stir in ham and chorizo.
Reserve 1 cup of beans.
Add the rest to the pot, along with the chipotle and garlic.
Mash the reserved beans.
Add to the pot.
Simmer beans until they become thick and soupy (about 30 minutes).
If the beans become too dry, stir in water.
Remove chipotle and garlic, and serve.

ROCHESTER WHITE HOTS MEAT SAUCE

Ingredients

½ lb. ground beef
1 Tablespoon minced onions
½ Teaspoon paprika
½ Teaspoon black pepper
¼ Teaspoon chili powder
¼ Teaspoon cayenne pepper
¼ Teaspoon ground cinnamon
¼ Teaspoon salt
Dash crushed thyme leaves
1 ¼ cups water

Directions

Place all ingredients in a small saucepan.
Add water.
Mix well.
Place saucepan over low heat,.
Cover and cook 1 ½ hours (at a very slow simmer).
Remove cover from saucepan.
Continue to simmer for another 1 ½ hours.
When done, the meat sauce will be a thin gravy, watery, but not dried out.

TUNNBRÖDSRULLE
(Swedish Hot Dog on Flat Bread)

Ingredients

8 extra-long, all-beef hot dogs
4 leaves of bib lettuce
4 large thin flat breads
4 cups of cooked mashed potatoes
2 cups small frozen cooked shrimp-thawed
½ cup finely chopped green onion

Sauce for shrimp salad:

1 cup sour crème
1 Teaspoon sugar
½ cup mayonnaise
1 Tablespoon of Dijon mustard
1 Tablespoon of ketchup
½ Tablespoon fresh finely chopped dill
Salt & Pepper
Tabasco sauce

Directions

Mix mayonnaise, sour cream, sugar, mustard, ketchup and dill.
Add salt, pepper and Tabasco sauce to taste.
Add drained shrimp to sauce and gently mix in.
Heat the hot dogs over a frying pan or grill.
Warm the mashed potatoes in a separate pan.
Place a leaf of lettuce onto *tunnbröd*/flat bread.
Top with a scoop of mashed potatoes.
Add a generous spoonful of the shrimp-salad
Add two hot dogs.
Top with a generous pinch of green onions.
Wrap the flat bread around the filling

Nota bene: Optionally, substitute two large, burrito-size tortillas.

SEATTLE CREAM CHEESE DOGS

Ingredients
¼ cup butter
1 Walla Walla or Vidalia (sweet onion), thinly sliced
1 (4 ounce) package cream cheese, or Neufchatel cheese.
4 hot dogs, or your favorite sausages
4 hot dog buns
Brown mustard
Sauerkraut (optional)
Thinly-sliced cucumbers (optional)

Directions
Melt butter in a skillet over medium heat.
Add onions.
Slowly cook until onions soften and turn deep brown (15 min).
Warm the cream cheese over low heat in skillet until very soft.
Preheat grill or grill pan to medium-high heat.
Lightly grill/toast hot dog buns on both sides.
Grill hot dogs until well browned.
To assemble, spread warm cream cheese on toasted bun.
Add hot dog or sausage.
Top with onions
Dress with mustard and sauerkraut.

SAUCE AMÉRICAINE

Ingredients

1/3 cup cognac
1/2 cup white wine
1/3 cup fish stock (substitute splash of clam juice)
4 cups shrimp shells (or fresh sea scallops sweet flavor)
6 garlic cloves, finely minced
4 shallots, thinly sliced
1/4 Teaspoon dried tarragon
1/8 Teaspoon cayenne pepper
1 pinch nutmeg
1 pinch ground ginger
1 pinch ground cloves
1/4 cup fresh tomato puree (or crushed canned tomatoes)
2 Teaspoons lemon juice
1/8 Teaspoon salt
1 dash Tabasco sauce

Directions

Coarsely chop up the shrimp shells.
Place chopped shells in a 5 quart, non-aluminum saucepan
Add cognac, wine, stock, garlic, shallots, herbs and spices.
Cover.
Cook over medium heat 15-20 minutes or until the shallots go limp.
Strain mixture through a fine sieve
Pressing down with a spoon to force all the liquid through.
Discard solids.
Return THE stock to a clean saucepan.
Stir tomato puree into stock.
Cook uncovered for five minutes, or until the sauce thickens slightly.

FLO'S HOT DOG RELISH

Ingredients
10 lbs. yellow onions, finely chopped
1 quart molasses
1 cup white vinegar
1 lb. brown sugar
1 ½ tablespoons crushed red pepper flakes
½ ounce Frank's red hot sauce

Directions
Food process or blend onions and crushed red peppers.
Chop fine.
Put all ingredients in a big kettle, and heat until it gets hot.
Stir frequently.
Simmer for eight hours.
Put in glass jars and store in fridge, or can.

SALSA ROSADA

Ingredients
½ cup mayonnaise adjust to taste
¼ cup ketchup
¼ Teaspoon lime juice
Salt and fresh ground pepper to taste
¼ Teaspoon Tabasco (Optional)
Cumin (optional)

Directions
Whisk together all the ingredients until well-blended.
Season with salt and pepper.

Nota Bene: Mixing mayonnaise and ketchup together in a ratio of two parts mayo to one part ketchup gives life to a flavourful sauce that's a tangy, sweet and fruity.

FLINT CONEY ISLAND SAUCE

Ingredients

1 Teaspoon butter

1 Teaspoon margarine

1 ½ pounds ground beef (not lean)

2 medium onions, finely chopped

1 clove garlic, crushed,

Salt and pepper to taste.

3 tablespoons mild paprika

2 tablespoons chili powder

1 Tablespoon mustard

3 tablespoons ground cumin

6 ounces tomato sauce

6 ounces water.

4 or 5 hot dogs, or ½ pound beef heart and kidney

Directions

Combine all the ingredients (except the hot dogs) in a heavy pan and cook over med to low heat until the mixture becomes dry and crumbly.

Do **not** brown the ground beef before adding to the sauce.

Simmer the sauce until thickened.

If too wet or greasy, add a few crumbled saltine crackers.

Stir occasionally to keep the ground beef from clumping.

Grind the hot dogs very fine, or chop fine in food processor.

Stir into the beef mixture

Simmer an additional 15 minutes.

Nota bene: The secret ingredient in this recipe is the ground hot dogs.

TRADITIONAL
FLINT CONEY ISLAND SAUCE

Ingredients
½ lb. Beef kidney, finely ground
½ lb. Beef heart, finely ground
¼ cup rendered beef suet or lard
3 Tablespoon of paprika
2 Tablespoon of chili powder
Kosher salt
Fresh ground pepper

Directions
Render the beef suet or lard.
Reserve.
In a large bowl mix all the ingredients except salt and pepper.
Gently crumble the meat mixture into a medium pot.
Add the melted fat and stir well.
Simmer over low heat for about 45 minutes.
Add suet or lard, as necessary, to prevent meat from drying out.

Nota Bene: No matter what the recipe, slow-cook the Coney dogs so the casing has snap.

JACKSON CONEY ISLAND SAUCE

Ingredients
1- ½pounds ground beef heart
1 Tablespoon vegetable oil
2 tsp. garlic salt
2 tsp. chili powder
2 tsp. cumin powder
2 tsp. paprika

Directions
Brown the meat in the vegetable oil.
Do not drain it.
Once browned, add the spices.
Add just enough water to moisten the sauce. (Scant few Tablespoons).
Stirring occasionally, simmer the sauce for about 30 minutes.
The goal is to reduce without drying it out.
Serve over grilled natural casings hot dogs
Preferred toppings are mustard and finely chopped onion.

A COMPENDIUM OF MARINADES

Unlike most marinades that tenderize meat, hot dog marinades do not tenderize, but rather, add flavor since the dogs are already very tender. All that's requires is cross-hatching or spiral cutting the dogs with shallow cuts down all sides, then marinating for several hours. Crosshatching, or spiraling, allows marinade to seep deeply into the hot dog and creates a larger surface area to come in contact with a searing-hot grill and gives the hot dog lots of little charred and crispy bits that taste wonderful.

Directions
Whisk together all of the ingredients, save out the hot dogs.
Cross cut or spiral cut each hot dog m
Place the hot dogs in a plastic bag along with the marinade
Agitate until completely coated.
Cover and refrigerate overnight.

Quick Marinade
¼ cup Golden Balsamic Vinegar
¼ cup Honey
2 tablespoons Whole Grain Mustard
4 Cloves Garlic
4 Hot Dogs

Soy-Sesame Marinade
½ cup ketchup,
2 tablespoons soy sauce,
1 Tablespoon red wine vinegar,
1 splash sesame oil,
1 splash Worcestershire sauce.

(Marinades continued on following page)

Garlic Marinade

2 tablespoons ketchup,
1 Tablespoon soy sauce,
½ Teaspoon vegetable oil,
1 large garlic clove, minced

Beer Marinade

½ cup olive oil,
1 cup dark beer,
¼ cup lemon juice,
4 cloves garlic, smashed,
1 ½ teaspoons sea salt,
1 Teaspoon freshly ground black pepper,
2 bay leaves,
1 Teaspoon dry mustard,
1 Teaspoon basil,
1 Teaspoon oregano,
1 Teaspoon thyme.

Creole marinade

¼ cup Creole seasoning, such as Tony Chachere's,
½ cup Worcestershire sauce.

MAKING MUSTARD

Making mustard is as simple as the sea is salt: Grind the seeds and add liquid. But the truth be told, there's more to the story for any chef who wishes to make great mustard, and not merely mustard.

Mustard seeds are ground into a powder then mixed with water and vinegar creating a chemical reaction that releases the enzyme myrosinae as well as various glucosinolates. It is this reaction that creates mustard's heat. There are three choices of mustard seed: White, brown and black. White mustard undergoes a different, milder reaction than do brown mustard or black mustard, which are far zingier. American yellow mustard is made with white mustard seed and turmeric, brown mustards are in most of the better mustards, and black mustard is in hot mustards or in Indian cuisine. Tame black and brown mustard seeds by soaking them overnight in water before grinding. Grind mustard seeds with a spice grinder or a mortar and pestle.

The best mustards combine brown or black mustard seeds with yellow mustard powder: The two sets of chemical reactions complement each other so as to synergistically create a more complex mustard flavor. Mustard husks may be ground with the seeds, or winnowed away after the initial crushing. Whole-grain mustard paste retains some unground or partially ground mustard seeds. Sometimes mustard is simmered to moderate its bite, and other times it is aged.

What gives mustard its characteristic bite is a chemical inside the seeds that reacts with cool or cold liquid. The seeds must be kibbled (broken) in order to unleash the fiery chemical. Heat damages this reaction. So naturally it follows in order to make a hot mustard use cold water, or warm water for mellow mustard. Similarly, mustard sauce loses its punch when cooked to long, so reserve a little extra fresh mustard to be added at the end of cooking.

Always add water, or a non-acidic liquid first. Let the mixture work for 10 minutes or so, then add the acid (vinegar, verjus, lemon juice). Salt to taste at a ratio of 1 to 2 teaspoons per cup of prepared mustard.

When adding liquids to ground mustard seed, know that the temperature makes a difference. Hot liquid lends a milder mustard, cold liquid lends more kick.

Left alone, mustard loses its bite in a few days, or even in just a few hours. Simply put, the longer mustard sits, the milder it gets. But adding acid (vinegar) or horseradish sets the reaction. Salt not only improves the flavor, but also helps preserve the mustard. Skip the vinegar and salt and the pasty condiment is still mustard, albeit one that won't t keep for very long. It won't go bad, but it will lose flavor. Made with salt and vinegar, mustard is nearly invulnerable to deterioration.

Because of its antibacterial properties, mustard does not require refrigeration. It will not grow mold, mildew, or harmful bacteria.

Mustard lasts indefinitely without becoming inedible. If it dries out, loses flavor, or turns brown from oxidation, the simple act of mixing in a small amount of wine or vinegar resurrects it.

ANCIENT ROMAN MUSTARD

(From the early 5th century Roman cookbook: *De re coquinaria*)

Ingredients (Ancient Recipe)
Ground mustard
Pepper
Caraway
Lovage
Grilled coriander

Ingredients #2 (Modern Variation)
1 cup black or brown mustard seeds
½ cup almonds, chopped
½ cup pine nuts, chopped
1 cup cold water
½ cup red wine vinegar
2-3 teaspoons salt

Directions
Grind whole mustard seeds for a few seconds in a spice or coffee
grinder, or crush with a mortar and pestle, left mostly whole.
Add the chopped nuts and grind into a paste. (optional ingredient).
Transfer ingredients to a bowl and add the salt and cold water.
Mix well and let stand for 10 minutes.
Pour in the vinegar and stir well.
Pour paste into a glass jar and store in the fridge.
Wait at least 24 hours before using.
Mustard made this way lasts several months in the fridge.

Nota bene: In this recipe the black mustard seeds, stronger than
American mustard, are balanced by the richness of the nuts.

COARSE GROUND MUSTARD

Ingredients

1/3 cup mustard seed

1/3 cup cider vinegar

1 clove garlic, halved

3 tablespoons water

3 tablespoons liquid honey

¼ Teaspoon salt

1 pinch ground cinnamon

Directions

Combine mustard seeds, vinegar and garlic in a small bowl.
Cover.

Refrigerate for 36 hours.

Discard the halved garlic cloves.

Process the mixture with water in a food processor until coarse.

Stir in honey, salt and cinnamon.

BASIC MUSTARD

Ingredients

¼ cup dry mustard powder

2 teaspoons light brown sugar (Optional)

1 Teaspoon kosher salt

½ Teaspoon turmeric

¼ Teaspoon paprika

¼ Teaspoon garlic powder

½ cup sweet pickle juice

¼ cup water

½ cup cider vinegar

¼ cup mustard seed

Directions

Whisk dry mustard, brown sugar, salt, turmeric, paprika and garlic powder together.

In a separate container, combine pickle juice, water and vinegar.

Grind mustard seed in a spice grinder or blender for a minimum of one to two minutes, occasionally pausing to pulse.

Add the mustard powder along with the other dry ingredients.

Add pickle juice, water and vinegar.

Whisk to combine.

Microwave on high for one minute.

Remove from the microwave.

Puree with a stick blender for one minute.

Pour into a glass jar or container.

Allow to cool uncovered.

Cover.

Refrigerate.

HOMEMADE MUSTARD

Ingredients
1/3 cup mustard seeds
1/3 cup white wine vinegar
1/3 cup dry white wine (or water)
1 Tablespoon maple syrup
1 Teaspoon ground turmeric
½ Teaspoon salt
Pinch of cayenne
2 to 4 tablespoons water, as needed.
1-3 teaspoons prepared horseradish (Optional).

Directions
Combine all ingredients, except horseradish.
Cover
Let stand for 2 to 3 days.
Grind in a blender to a smooth consistency.
Add two to four tablespoons of water if the mustard is too thick.
Blend in the horseradish.

Nota bene: Turmeric lends this mustard its lively, school bus yellow color.

SWEDISH SHRIMP SALAD
(Skagenröra)

Ingredients
1 pound fresh, cooked shrimp
3 Tablespoon mayo
3 Tablespoon crème fraîche or sour cream
3 Tablespoon fresh dill finely chopped
1 Tablespoon of finely chopped red onion
1 tsp. lemon juice
Scant few drops of hot sauce
Pinch of Salt
Freshly ground white pepper

Directions
Peel and devein the shrimp.
Bring a pot of salted water to a simmer over medium-high heat.
Add the shrimp.
Poach until just cooked through, about three to four minutes.
Drain shrimp in a colander.
Transfer to a bowl of ice water in order to halt cooking.
When using frozen shrimp, make sure they're fully thawed.
With fresh-cooked or frozen-thawed, pat dry with a paper towel,
otherwise the salad will be too watery.
Combine the crème fraiche, dill, onion, lemon juice and zest.
Add the shrimp to the mayo conglomeration.
Toss, making sure all of the shrimps are evenly coated.
Season with salt and pepper.

Nota Bene: Medium cold water shrimp the size of a doll's hand, are
the best choice for this recipe. The bigger, jumbo shrimp lack flavor,
and the smallest can be on the mushy.

NORWEGIAN SHRIMP SALAD
(Rejesalat)

Ingredients

1 pound cooked, deveined small shrimp
4 thin slices canned pineapple, diced
½ cup mayonnaise
¼ cup ketchup
½ – 1 Teaspoon curry

Directions

Pat shrimp dry with a paper towel.
Finely dice shrimp and pineapple.
Add mayonnaise, ketchup and curry.
Stir gently to combine.
Refrigerate before serving.

"I just made some hot dogs. I just ate some hot dogs. I love hot dogs!" **- Bradford Macy Eaton**

GLOSSARY

Aioli - is a Mediterranean sauce made of garlic and olive oil, and in some regions, other emulsifiers such as egg. In the Spanish province of Catalan and across the border in French, Provençal, its name means garlic and oil in. And in Spain, purists consider that the absence of egg is what distinguishes aioli from mayonnaise, however this is not so true in France. True aioli contains no other seasoning than garlic.

Asian Snack Mix - A slightly spicy blend of peanuts, rice crackers, almonds, wasabi peas, and cashews.

Boston Brown Bread – Boston brown bread is steamed in cans as opposed to being baked in an oven. Slightly sweet, it's made with a mixture of fours including cornmeal, rye, whole wheat, graham flour, and from the addition of sweeteners like molasses and maple syrup and raisins. Leavening most comes from baking soda (sodium bicarbonate) Seasonal, it is most commonly served in fall and winter, and is frequently served with baked beans.

Charro Beans – Mexican pork and beans.

Chipotle - from the Nahuatl word *chilpoctli*, which means smoked chili. This is a smoke-dried jalapeño. A chipotle's heat is similar to that of the Espelette pepper, jalapeño, Guajillo chili, Hungarian wax pepper, Anaheim pepper, and Tabasco sauce. Varieties vary in size and heat. In Mexico, the jalapeño is also known as the *cuaresmeño* and *gordo.*

Chirmol – Is a classic Guatemalan condiment, a tomato-based salsa. Traditionally, the sauce is used on carne asada, but can be applied in place of salsa on any dish including hot dogs. Chirmol pairs well with seafood and makes an interesting twist on a classic shrimp cocktail. Chirmol is Mayan for running nose.

Cold Slaw - The word coleslaw comes from the Dutch, but Texans renamed it **cold** slaw and re-invented it by omitting mayonnaise from the list of ingredients. To make it, toss Crunchy cabbage, cucumbers and peppers along with an onion-turmeric vinaigrette. Because it is made without mayonnaise, it is a favorite summer picnic salad that survives without refrigeration for hours.

Coleslaw - means cabbage salad. Slaw is shorthand for coleslaw.

Comal - Is a smooth, flat griddle typically used in Mexico and Central America to cook tortillas, toast spices, to sear meat.

Condiment - A spice, sauce, or preparation added to food to impart a particular flavor, to enhance its flavor. Originally the term described pickled or preserved foods, but the meaning has changed over the years to the point where the exact definition of what is and is not a condiment varies. For example, cheese is considered a condiment in some European countries.

Cotija - is a hard cow's milk cheese named after Cotija, Michoacán, Mexico. Cotija comes in two primary versions. El queso Cotija de Montaña or grain cheese, is dry and firm, with little taste other than its saltiness, several times saltier than typical cheese, for preservation. Tajo cheese is a moister, fattier, and less salty version that holds its shape when cut, with a flavor similar to Greek feta.

Düsseldorf Mustard - a strong mustard, with a creamy consistency and a malt brown color, served in a traditional pot called *Mostertpöttche*. Dusseldorf mustard is blended with both brown and yellow mustard seeds, unfiltered spirit vinegar (produced in Dusseldorf), the special lime and mineral rich water of Dusseldorf, salt, sugar and spices. The soul of mustard is the paste containing tiny pieces of triple ground mustard seek husks that lend it a hot, malty, spicy flavour. Düsseldorf Mustard can be either a smooth brown or grainy. Close your eyes and from its flavour one might confuse it was a very strong Dijon.

Five-spice powder - is a mixture of five or more spices used primarily in Chinese/Asian cuisine. While there are many variants, common ingredients include: Star anise, cloves, Chinese cinnamon, Sichuan pepper and fennel seeds.

Fromager d'Affinois- is a French double-cream soft cheese made from cow's milk, similar to Brie in production, appearance and flavour. It is produced by the Fromagerie Guilloteau Company.

Guasacaca - A Venezuelan avocado-based sauce, lighter and more flavorful than Mexican guacamole.

Ketcepes - Is a mushroom-based catsup.

Ketchup – Tomato ketchup on a hot dog? You've got to be kidding!

Kibble - To crush or grind coarsely, as in kibbled mustard seeds.

Pease Pudding - Pease pudding is thick, mild-tasting, pudding made of boiled, split yellow peas or Carlin peas, with water, salt, and spices and often cooked with a bacon or ham joint. It's a key ingredient in classic saveloy dip which consists of a bread roll smeared with a healthy dollop of pease pudding on one half, sage and onion stuffing on the other with a slight smear of mustard, and a saveloy sausage cut in half and dipped gently into either the stock that the saveloys are boiled in, or gravy. Only the top half is dipped so as to not make it difficult to hold while eating.

Piccalilli - Is an English interpretation of Indian pickles, a relish of chopped pickled vegetables and spices. Regional recipes vary considerably.

A Pie Floater - is an Australian meat pie sitting in, and sometimes submerged or even inverted in, a bowl of thick pea soup. Usually purchased in the street from pie-carts as a late evening meal.

Piquillo pepper - is a variety of chili, *capsicum annuum*, having a sweet taste with no heat, traditionally grown in Northern Spain near the town of Lodosa. Short-statured, just three-inches long, its name derives from the Spanish language word for little beak.

Rémoulade (Danish) - Has a mild, sweet-sour taste and a medium yellow color. The typical industrially-made variety does not contain capers, but finely-chopped cabbage and pickled cucumber, fair amounts of sugar and hints of mustard, cayenne pepper, coriander and onion, and turmeric for color. The herbs are replaced by herbal essences, e.g., tarragon vinegar. Starch, gelatin or milk protein may be added as thickeners. Homemade or gourmet varieties may use olive oil (especially good with fish), capers, pickles, carrots, cucumber, lemon juice, dill, chervil, parsley or other fresh herbs, and possibly curry. In Denmark Rémoulade is mostly used for open sandwiches with cold meatballs or fried fish and of course, hot dogs.

Roulade - is a condiment invented in France, usually aioli- or mayonnaise-based. Although similar to tartar sauce, it is often more yellowish (or reddish in Louisiana), sometimes flavored with curry, and sometimes contains chopped pickles or piccalilli. It can also contain horseradish, paprika, anchovies, capers and a host of other items. While its original purpose was possibly for serving with meats, it is now more often used as an accompaniment to seafood dishes, especially pan-fried breaded fish fillets (primarily sole and plaice) and seafood cakes (such as

112

crab or salmon cakes).

Requeijão - Brazilian cream cheese, is white in color but dissimilar to American cream cheese. Requeijão is a loose, ricotta-like cheese used to make cheese spreads. A mild, unsalty ricotta can be substituted. This variety is most often sold in the markets wrapped in fresh corn husks. *Catupiry,* a soft, mild-tasting cheese, is one of the most popular requeijão brands in Brazil. Its name derives from the Tupi word meaning excellent.

Sauce Américaine - is a recipe from classic French cookery containing chopped onions, tomatoes, white wine, brandy, salt, cayenne pepper, butter and fish stock. Modern recipes usually add tarragon and use lobster stock rather than pounded lobster and often replace cayenne pepper with paprika. Arguably one of the greatest creations of the French kitchen, no one is certain exactly who created this flavorful sauce or how it came by its name. That said, gastronomic experts generally agree that the name does translate to mean in the American style, and neither was it created in the United States of America. Instead it is believed to have originated in Provence for the simple fact it boasts the taste distinctions of the region and the characteristic use of tomatoes, garlic and olive oil.

Salsa Rosada - Also known as golf sauce, or *salsa coctel,* a popular Latin American sauce made with mix of mayonnaise and ketchup

Sport Peppers - Are tasty, medium-hot, bite-sized and packed in seasoned brine to lend a spicy crunch. They contain virtually no fat and boast a mere five calories per pepper.

Tzatziki - is a sauce made of salted strained yogurt from either sheep or goat milk mixed with cucumbers, garlic, salt, olive oil, sometimes with vinegar or lemon juice, and herbs like dill, mint, parsley, thyme and the like. It is always served cold. Often associated with Gyros, it's not only tastes great on hot dog, it is also low-carb, Keto, gluten-free, low-glycemic.

Utah Fry Sauce - A simple combination of ketchup and mayonnaise (two to one ratio of Mayo to ketchup) renowned as dipping sauce for French fries. The Utah-based burger chain Arctic Circle claims to have invented fry sauce in the 1940s. No matter, the practice of combining ketchup and mayonnaise is hardly a unique idea, as the condiment is known by various names around the world.

In Argentina fry sauce is called Salsa Golf. In Germany it's Rott Weiss or Red White. Variations on the theme combine ketchup and mayo with small amounts of mustard, garlic, lemon juice, and/or hot sauce. Beware of restaurants attempting to pass off bottled Thousand Island dressing as fry sauce. While similar, they are not the same.